unshackled

the dustbin of donald trump

phil dellio & scott woods

unshackled

the dustbin of donald trump

front cover design: valerie mais

"And never hit bottom and keep falling through,
Just relaxed and paying attention"

— "5D (Fifth Dimension)," the Byrds (1966)

Phil and Scott dedicate this book to 2008.

contents

Introduction

Roughly speaking, there are two kinds of people in the world: those who see connections and similarities everywhere, and those who are quick to point out the ten thousand ways those connections and similarities immediately break down when you take a closer look at them. This book is for that first group of people.

Almost from the moment that Donald Trump began the odyssey that would end with his surreal election as the 45th President of the United States, journalists, political commentators, and cultural critics struggled to explain what was happening by looking far and wide for historical precedents, connections that would make sense of something that seemed to make no sense at all. One of the first and best attempts to do so—and to a degree the inspiration for this book—was a piece Frank Rich wrote for *New York* magazine in September of 2015, "Donald Trump Is Saving Our Democracy." (The title, while it wasn't exactly meant ironically, did require some context.) The first Republican primary was still three months away when Rich's piece appeared, but for weeks Trump had been sitting atop a freakishly large Republican field in all polling, and he had already established a discombobulating pattern of creating a major commotion (e.g., his sketchy medical insights into some pointed questioning from moderator Megyn Kelly following the first Republican debate) and emerging from the wreckage not only still intact, but seemingly stronger than ever. "As the summer of Donald Trump came to its end," Rich wrote, "and the prospect of a springtime for Trump no longer seemed like a gag, the quest to explain the billionaire's runaway clown car went into overdrive."

So Rich gathered together some of those early explanations—Joe McCarthy, Ross Perot, Hugo Chávez—and went looking for others. Clearly the search couldn't be limited to the world of politics and politicians; Trump, a product of junky celebrity and obscene wealth and reality television, sent Rich in the direction of movies (*Nashville, Bulworth, Bob Roberts*), comedians (Stephen Colbert, Don Rickles), and Terry Southern's 1959 novel *The Magic Christian*, which "anticipated just the kind of ruckus a Trump could make." Maybe Trump's ascension wasn't as baffling and as unprecedented—and, by implication, as frightening—as it initially seemed. Maybe he was the logical endpoint of a perverse and fragmentary story that had been unfolding for decades. You had to piece it together, but maybe it had been hiding in plain view all along.

Sparked by Rich's piece, we started looking for other clues that would help answer the most basic question of all: How did Trump happen? We definitely weren't the only ones: How-did-Trump-happen? pieces soon became an industry unto itself, with pieces appearing by the dozens that found portents of Trump scattered across a half-century (and sometimes beyond) of cultural and political loose ends. (To help you wade through the deluge, if you're interested, we've included an extensive bibliography of relevant online pieces, plus a short list of Trump-related material we bypassed for one reason or another.) As we went about compiling our own list, it was difficult to stay ahead of not only everyone else's detective work, but also, especially in the last few weeks of the campaign, events themselves—we found ourselves reworking entries on Howard Stern, *The Apprentice*, Miss Universe, and others to account for last-minute developments that upended the campaign.

Connections—we like them, and we see them everywhere. As Trump took hold of the media landscape in the fall of 2015, and then dominated it for the next 12 months like nothing anyone had ever seen (even Obama in 2008 shared at least some of the spotlight with Hillary Clinton and Sarah Palin), it felt as if there were Trumps lurking somewhere within everything we put to the test. Oddball indie singer-songwriter Mojo Nixon once wrote a song about that kind of omnipresent stranglehold on the popular imagination: "Elvis Is Everywhere" he observed back in 1987, which itself became one of the artifacts Greil Marcus assembled four years later for his book *Dead Elvis: A Chronicle of a Cultural Obsession*. And that's what we've rounded up here: the contours of a cultural obsession, over a hundred people, movies, and miscellaneous ephemera that for one reason or another felt to us like doorways to Trump.

How visible these doorways are will vary from entry to entry and from reader to reader. We think most will make sense immediately—at least one, Lonesome Rhodes from Elia Kazan's 1957 film *A Face in the Crowd*, has been cited by so many other Trump-watchers that you half-expected Andy Griffith's phony populist to step out Kazan's film and turn up on CNN one night as a Trump surrogate. Other entries connect to Trump at a more oblique angle, but keep an open mind and we think they'll come into focus too. Now and again, we let pure instinct guide us. We won't try too strenuously to sell you on the idea that Camille Paglia or Morrie the wig salesman from *Goodfellas* anticipated the candidacy of Donald Trump, but we do think you can find them somewhere along the road to Trump if you look hard enough. One of our guiding principles in writing this book was to avoid, for the most part, Trump's own stated influences, but rather to imagine what combined cultural, political, and psychological particles the Trump universe is made up of. What Trump has said or what he thinks about all that follows (or whether he's even aware of some of what we write about—*Citizen Kane* is supposedly his favourite film, a rather startling breach in the space-time continuum) is not something we tried to pin down.

When we started putting this together in early August, just after the conventions, there was still something vaguely—let us emphasize that: *vaguely*—resembling a normal election going on. The two candidates went into the conventions with Trump behind two or three points, Clinton doubled that coming out of them, and then the lead narrowed again as the debates approached. More than half the book was written during those three weeks, and without really adopting any kind of co-ordinated strategy (we wrote separately, adding new names to our master list as they occurred to us), we both continued to write about Trump as we'd always seen him: fascinating, often ridiculous, sometimes very funny in a train-wreck sort of way (in those early Republican debates, we suspect a lot more people on the left enjoyed Trump's antics than would ever admit it—he was insulting and running circles around other *Republicans*), sometimes not at all (mocking *New York Times* reporter Serge Kovaleski, ugh), clearly ill-prepared to run a general-election campaign, but unpredictable enough—and facing a flawed enough candidate on the other side—that who could say for sure, maybe he'd somehow manage to win. (If he actually wanted to, that is—that was part of the fascination.) It still felt like you could say, or even think, those words—"Maybe he'll somehow win"—without actually attaching any meaning to them. Because obviously he couldn't.

From the debates forward, things changed. More than once. Trump himself didn't change, not exactly—when you announce your campaign with an entrance worthy of Liberace, and then proceed to issue dire warnings about Mexican rapists taking over the country, there's not a lot of room below for a downward spiral—but concrete events (the *Access Hollywood* tape, the procession of corroborating women, Trump's behaviour in the debates and at the Al Smith dinner) made it harder and harder for us to not just want to join most of the rest of the world and forget Trump ever happened. Critical mass was reached somewhere in that last month; we weren't as sure anymore that those connections that made him so interesting to us in the first place were still worth pursuing, and the schadenfreude we thrilled to in those early Republican debates—the karmic perfection of watching the party's id unleashed and devouring itself—had gotten immeasurably uglier. Low-Energy Jeb felt like a lifetime ago. So we had to go back and adjust tone here and there, especially in some of the entries we wrote early on. And then, on Nov. 9, we had to start adjusting again.

So we're putting this out in very different circumstances than we ever envisioned. But no matter how sobering the prospects for the next four years are, or how demoralizing any reconstruction of the past year-and-a-half might be, we think there's still a jigsaw puzzle in there worth assembling—a compelling one, even if all the pieces don't fit. Besides, much like Trump in the early hours of Nov. 9, when someone sidled up to him and whispered into his ear "Um...you *won*," there's not much else we can do at this point except go forward.

Index of Entries

trumps like us

(a rough rough-draft of history;
good people and bad people
who cleared the way)

Sarah Palin – Where to begin? More than any single person we write about in these pages, it was Sarah Palin who prepared the world for Donald Trump, presidential candidate. John McCain's strange, Hail-Mary pick for VP seemed like a stroke of genius for a brief moment in August of 2008; the Alaskan governor's convention speech caused a sensation (pit bull with lipstick and all that), and McCain took the lead in an election that shouldn't have even been competitive. And then, as is standard practice in political campaigns, Palin spoke some more (even with a major effort to hide her in the hills of Wasilla), and the more she said—she was the blueprint for Trump's pure-id, stream-of-consciousness ramblings—the clearer it became that she had no earthly clue what she was saying, why she was saying it, or what the job she was applying for might entail. In a joint endorsement appearance with Trump last January, she reminded everyone what crazy sounded like pre-Trump: "Looking around at all of you, you hardworking Iowa families. You farm families, and teachers, and teamsters, and cops, and cooks. You rockin' rollers. And holy rollers! All of you who work so hard. You full-time moms. You with the hands that rock the cradle. You all make the world go round, and now our cause is one." It might have been the one time during the entire 2016 election when Trump looked mortified by the historical tackiness of his own campaign.

Rob Ford – When Trump began his astounding takeover of the Republican Party during the summer of 2015, a few of the first articles to appear that tried to place him historically focused on the notorious, scandal-ridden ex-mayor of Toronto (at a time when Ford was still alive). The parallels were obvious: the bullying, uncouth, blustery rhetoric; the brand identification with a single slogan ("Make America Great Again" being

Trump's version of Ford's "Stop the Gravy Train") in place of the more mundane details of governance; the loyalty of working-class citizens who felt neglected and condescended to by politicians across the spectrum; the master-class in media manipulation; and the moneyed father and privileged background that didn't necessarily fit into the rest of the narrative so well. Trump was tweeting enthusiastically about Ford as early as 2013, when he still only had 43 followers: "Who would you rather have negotiating with Iran—President Obama or Toronto Mayor Ford?" (Take a few seconds and try to get your head around that.) It was fitting then, in the wake of the *Access Hollywood* tape, that Rob's brother Doug was one of the people who stepped forward to defend Trump: "I have four girls and my wife. So I have five women. I asked them, 'Does this bother you what happened eleven years ago?' And all of them—I didn't coerce them or anything—they all said, 'We care about the taxes. We care about our business taxes going up under President Obama.'" Small sample size aside, the issue of Obama's reckless behaviour towards Canadian women had been waiting there all along for someone to bring it out into the open.

Rick Santelli / Michelle Bachmann – Before Trump finished the job, the Tea Party's splintering of the Republican Party during Barack Obama's first term—it was a phenomenon born out of an intense loathing for both the bank bailouts and Obama himself—served as an early warning that the Reagan coalition of economic, social, and foreign-policy conservatives was starting to fray. Santelli, a CNBC reporter, helped get things started in 2009 when he delivered a highly agitated on-air rant from the floor of the Chicago Mercantile Exchange excoriating Congress for assisting underwater homeowners; Bachmann ("Our movement at its core is an intellectual movement") soon became one of the first office holders to jump on board. The 2010 congressional mid-terms were a huge success for the Republican Party, although how much the fledgling Tea Party had to do with that—some of the candidates they endorsed won, some didn't—remains a little murky. Bachmann, meanwhile, only lasted six or seven minutes when she ran for the Republican nomination in 2012, and by and large you don't hear a great deal about the Tea Party these days. Whatever was left of it in 2016 seemed to migrate effortlessly into Trump's orbit.

Orly Taitz – "Do you know that Hawaii has a statute, 338, that allows foreign-born children of Hawaiian residence to get Hawaiian birth certificates? Did you know that?" This Obama-hating dentist/lawyer/real estate agent/failed politician—there's a joke in there somewhere—caused an uproar in 2009 when she produced, in the midst of five lawsuits she was handling against the president, a Kenyan birth certificate that would vindicate once and for all the "Birther" movement questioning Obama's citizenry and, by extension, his legitimacy as president. The birth certificate was revealed to be a complete fraud, and Birtherism started to fade back into the margins until it was resurrected in 2011 by a New York real-estate magnate contemplating a presidential bid: "I have people that actually have been studying it, and they cannot believe what they're finding." What we didn't know at the time, and what Trump has since clarified, is that he in fact did the President a solid by keeping the story alive for another five years.

Rush Limbaugh / Sean Hannity / Mark Levin – If there's one flashpoint of general consensus as to What Paved the Way for Trump, it's the aggrieved universe of right-wing talk radio.

Limbaugh, Hannity, and Levin—the first two unquestionably the most influential practitioners of the form, patronized by fiercely loyal audiences; many others could also be listed—get to where they're going in decidedly different ways. Limbaugh favours a kind of staccato, laconic sarcasm, delivered in a voice laced with theatrical incredulity; Hannity throws out a steady, rapid-fire itinerary of half- and quarter-truths (with some complete fabrications mixed in for variety) that makes your head spin; Levin's off on his own planet, but every now and again he works himself into a grunge-like froth (first the quiet part, now here comes the loud part) and starts hanging up on callers for being "big dummies." What links them, and several others, to Trump has been their decades-long project of cajoling their listeners into a permanent state of rage, disgust, and resentment—meant to be directed at the other side, but, as Trump proved in the primaries, sometimes you lose control of your audience and Pop Will Eat Itself. Limbaugh and Hannity's support for Trump became more and more unwavering through the last few weeks of the campaign, with Limbaugh, as he did during both Obama elections, sensing something monumentally exciting underfoot out there that he couldn't quite quantify. Most every poll couldn't seem to quantify it either. Which brings us to the three most difficult words we've had to utter in our entire lives: Limbaugh was right.

"Mr. Vaughn, what we are dealing with here is a perfect engine, an eating machine. It's really a miracle of evolution. All this machine does is swim and eat and make little sharks, and that's all."
   - Matt Hooper, *Jaws* (1975)

Alex Jones – The de facto leader of the America-is-burning conspiracy wing of America circa right-now, whose agitated, lozenge-free jeremiads target all shapes and sizes of beltway and insider reprobates. A 9/11 Truther with ratings that rival Rush Limbaugh's (a large but even quieter outpost of the silent majority), Jones, like Trump, seemingly raises a ruckus every time he clears his throat, and some of his inside-job theories surpass even Trump's Birtherism for indigestible lunacy (for instance, his positing of the Sandy Hook massacre of 2014, in which 28 people were murdered, as a government-perpetrated optical illusion—or in his words, a "hoax"). One of Jones's more popular news flashes was his 2009 claim that he discovered FEMA concentration camps, installed, naturally, by Barack Obama to round up U.S. dissidents. Rhetorically, the camps were of a piece with Trump's proposed giant wall, the only discernible difference being that one was supposedly here already, and was very very bad, while the other was supposedly on the way, and would be very very good (extremely very good, in fact—absolutely terrific, greatest development ever known to mankind, etc.).

Ann Coulter – Where there's a liberal or a leftist there's an Ann Coulter exposé following closely behind, and from a certain vantage point the anti-L-word bias of her printed screeds is comically imaginative: *Liberal Lies About the American Right*, *Liberal "Victims" and their Assault on America*, *Never Trust a Liberal Over 3—Especially a Republican*. In her two most recent tomes, 2015's *Adios America: The Left's Plan to Turn Our Country into a Third World Hellhole* (which Trump declared "a great read") and—brace yourself—2016's *In Trump We Trust: E Pluribus Awesome*, the root cause of Coulter's obsession comes to the fore, as noted on the back cover of the latter: "The combined vote for Trump and Cruz is a ringing chorus of what this party wants: a wall, deportation, and a lot less immigration, especially from Muslim countries. In other words, what the party wants is the diametric opposite of what Washington wants..." With the sort of timing you can't base a credible movie script around, *In Trump We Trust* hit bookstores the very day Trump hit the trail with his wall "softening" tour (which, to be fair, and depending on who said what and on which network, was also characterized as a "hardening"). Though Coulter initially lashed out on Twitter at Trump's apparent turnabout, she fell back in line soon enough, i.e., within five minutes or so, and decided that such wobbly triangulation on the part of Trump was no greater a concern than his previous 25 years or so of small-L bloviating on matters such as abortion, healthcare, and gun control. Consistency is for losers, right?

alt-right – The next-level grassroots successor to the Tea Party (and, stretching several decades back, the John Birch Society), alt-right is an amorphous, lower-case, platform-free movement—or anti-movement, as it were—whose associations with Trump, while difficult to pin down, are real enough (and even realer, according to some accounts, with regards to Donald Trump Jr.). Roughly in existence since (surprise) 2008, many of the ideas which have emerged from the alt-right play directly into Trump's canny exploitation of aggrieved whiteness. Alt-righters—think tank intellectuals and Twitter trolls alike— mince no words about their obsession with skin tone in the 21st century; some refer to themselves as "race realists," others belong to "human biodiversity" movements, all seem to agree that traditional conservatives, in their deference to social trends and human decency, have done more to beleaguer the white, western male than their mushy melting pot advocates on the left. Alt-righters' means of conveying all this, while certainly more extreme and prankish than Trump's, are nevertheless cut from a similar cloth: use social media (Twitter, especially) to antagonize and mock your enemies; rather than hiding from your contradictions and hypocrisies, wave those freak flags high (let your critics try to figure it out); never concede an inch on your right to say what you want when you want and to whom (in the alt-right universe, political correctness is the #1 scourge of humanity). Though the phrase "alt-right" may not have passed Trump's lips on the campaign trail, his hiring in August 2016 of Stephen Bannon from Breitbart Media (which functions as a house organ for much noxious alt-right ideology) signalled, if nothing else, an unwillingness on the candidate's behalf to back down on a year's worth of volatile race-baiting. Certainly, the line separating alt-right sentiments about race (such as spearheading alt-rightist Richard Spencer's call for "the creation of a White Ethno-State on the North American continent") and Trump provocations like "they send over rapists" or "look at my African-American" is a thin one indeed.

"The Unspoken Thing; Kesey's role and the whole direction the Pranksters were taking—all the Pranksters were conscious of it, but none of them put it into words, as I say. They made a point of not putting it into words. That in itself was one of the unspoken rules. *If you label it* this, *then it can't be* that..."
    - Tom Wolfe, *The Electric Kool-Aid Acid Test* (1968)

Newt Gingrich – Insurgent (Gingrich led the Republican's seismic takeover of Congress in 1994), Angry White Man (famously snarling at CNN's John King in one of the 2012 Republican debates), and expert media manipulator (keeping his cash-strapped candidacy afloat through debates and his ubiquity on the Sunday-morning panel shows), Gingrich provided a dry run for Trump four years ago when he briefly took his waning political celebrity—he seemed to relish the way interviewers still called him "Mr. Speaker"—and almost hijacked the 2012 Republican nomination. Famous for his endless supply of really strange ideas: pass Dickensian child labour laws, gerrymander the climate, install colonies and light sabres and energy-efficient mirrors in space. Besides running interference for Trump at the 2016 Republican convention, where he attempted to smooth over Ted Cruz's heretical non-endorsement, Gingrich also served as an unofficial adviser throughout the campaign. "If Trump keeps learning, he could become a big asset. He will shatter the traditional patterns." We missed the part where "if" happened, but "will" had a life of its own.

Chris Christie / Rudy Giuliani – Law-and-order tough guys from the East, Tony Soprano in Jersey vs. Johnny Sack in New York, and two of Trump's earliest and staunchest supporters. Both were front-runners themselves at different points in time to lead the Republicans into a general election. Giuliani, still a party favourite for his prominence during 9/11 as "America's Mayor" (noun, verb, etc.), led most early polling for the 2008 nomination, but his socially liberal positions, some puzzling strategy (like treating early primaries lightly), and a variety of scandals back in New York led to an early exit. Christie, meanwhile, basically *was* Donald Trump heading into the 2016 contest—brash, headstrong, prone to bullying and ridiculing his opponents; all those character traits thought of as "backbone"—but except for the endlessly replayed debate clip where he lay waste to Marco Rubio's campaign in a couple of minutes ("There it is, everybody, the memorized 25-second speech..."), Christie couldn't out-bully the real thing. Both men were also viewed within their party with a degree of suspicion that the ideologically-erratic Trump somehow dodged— Giuliani for being pro-choice, Christie for nuzzling President Obama on a tarmac once. Giuliani and Christie went all in with Trump once he secured the nomination, and while both were seen as likely cabinet appointees if Trump somehow managed to win, most viewed their unshakable allegiance as sure-fire career-killers. Seems like things will work out okay for Giuliani, but let us dispel once and for all with the notion that Chris Christie knows exactly what he's doing. He doesn't—he doesn't have a clue.

Boris Johnson – Following the U.K.'s decision in the spring of 2016 to leave the European Union, U.S. commentators on all sides of the political divide were quick to pounce on the theory that the startling Brexit referendum results presaged a Trump victory come November. Certainly, the outcome had flashes of a Make Britain Great Again-style revolt, fueled by political and economic unrest, bad faith (in the form of an anti-immigrant smear campaign), and a ridiculous mop of hair—the latter belonging to then-Mayor of London, Boris Johnson, one of the principle figureheads behind the Brexit campaign. Johnson, however, had more Trump in him than mere follicle disarray. On April 22 he penned an editorial in a British tabloid, dredging up a story about how Obama removed a bust of Winston Churchill from the Oval Office on the first day of his presidency (a premise which most commentators agreed was a smokescreen for Johnson's real beef, which was Obama's plea for Great Britain to stay in the E.U.). To drive the point home, Johnson threw down the Birther card, suggesting the statue removal "was a symbol of the part-Kenyan President's ancestral dislike of the British empire." And as if to further cement his spiritual kinship with Trumpism, Johnson afterward refused to back down on the claim, despite much howling among the U.K. press corps and across social media. Trump, somewhat obliquely (he claimed not to know who Johnson was), reciprocated by praising the Brexit results the morning after the referendum. Speaking from the 9th hole at Trump Turnberry, his Scottish golf resort (where his private jet just happened to be flying by that morning), the candidate praised the decision as "a great thing," informed the audience that he himself predicted the results, and noted at least one fringe benefit as a result: "When the pound goes down more people come to Turnberry."

"Do you think it's a personal matter with me, this boy? Are you telling me I see things in terms of personal pique? Don't you see that today that boy wiped his feet on the choice, on the predilections of sixty million men and women of the greatest country in the world...It was not me he criticized— it was my readers."
  – J.J. Hunsecker, *Sweet Smell of Success* (1957)

Pat Buchanan – A jarring indicator that George H.W. Bush's 1992 re-election bid would not end well came right out of the gate in New Hampshire, where hard-right pundit and former Nixon speechwriter Pat Buchanan won almost 40% of the vote against a sitting president whose approval rating, post-Gulf

War, had peaked at 90% only a year ago. Buchanan would dog Bush for the remainder of the primaries, steadily drawing support between 20-30% in most states, enough to (reluctantly) earn him a prime-time speaking slot at the convention. "There is a religious war going on in our country for the soul of America," Buchanan ominously warned. "It is a cultural war, as critical to the kind of nation we will one day be as was the Cold War itself." He sounded scary, and Bush went on to lose the election handily to Bill Clinton. When Trump came along 25 years later with a recycled version of Buchanan's hard-right nationalism, Buchanan sounded bemused and a little hurt at first: "I was relatively astonished when he came out against trade and immigration, and to Make America First—that's on my (campaign) hats!" With time Buchanan was able to put the hat slight behind him, though, blogging his support for Trump for the remainder of the election.

George Wallace – The segregationist Governor of Alabama's presidential campaigns in 1964 (as a Democrat), 1968 (independent), and 1972 (Democrat again) were a blueprint for Trump at the outer limits of his belligerence, incendiary rhetoric, and recklessness, and he caused the same ruptures and embarrassment within his own party that Trump triggered within his. "Segregation now, segregation tomorrow, segregation forever" was Wallace's version of Trump's Wall, and in 1968 he scrambled up the election in ways that made both parties nervous: Republicans were worried he'd split the Southern anti-civil rights (racist) vote, Democrats that he'd split the labour vote. In the end, he became the last independent ever to win electoral votes (46, winning five Southern states), leaving behind a slogan that outsiders and insurgents take as a first cause: "There's not a dime's worth of difference between the Republicans and Democrats." Trump himself seemed very conflicted on that point, switching party affiliation four or five times over the years before discovering the same thing Jerry did in his search for the perfect girlfriend on *Seinfeld*: he'd been looking for the Party of Me all along.

Barry Goldwater – At a turbulent juncture in American history—JFK's assassination a year removed, Vietnam coming onto the radar, civil rights tensions on the verge of exploding—hard-right activists, especially young Republicans, revolted and handed the 1964 nomination to Goldwater, running roughshod over the party establishment's desire for Nelson Rockefeller when such hidden-hand power still held sway. Goldwater's combative rhetoric ("extremism in the defense of liberty is no vice") and reputation as a quick-draw loose cannon who couldn't be trusted with the nuclear codes (the Hillary ad where dumbfounded children react to crude Trump soundbites echoed Lyndon Johnson's infamous daisy ad) made Goldwater an easy mark for Democrats, who went on to win their last presidential landslide ever. This year was supposed to be that year all over again.

Joe McCarthy – As was the case with the Wisconsin senator who ripped the country apart in the early 1950s, it was Trump's penchant for conspiracy and innuendo that provided his most visible entry-point into national politics when he resurrected the whole Birther pseudo-controversy in the spring of 2011: "Why doesn't he show his birth certificate? I want to see his birth certificate." That particular avenue, by then on its third or fourth go-around, was squashed yet again, most witheringly by the president himself at that year's Correspondents Dinner ("You fired Gary Busey...these are the kind of decisions that would keep me up at night"). But time and again throughout this year's election, Trump brandished a newer version of McCarthy's cherished list of 200-and-counting known Communists employed by the U.S. Government: his vague assertions that "Many people are saying" this, that, and the other—phantom issues ranging from Hillary's health to links between her and Iran—without ever specifying exactly who or how many. (The lasting influence of Roy Cohn, McCarthy's chief counsel who would later serve as Trump's lawyer and mentor, undoubtedly helped shape Trump's conspiratorial mindset.) Trump was even called out by his own personal Joseph Welch at one point when, replying to one of Trump's petulant outbursts, an exasperated Anderson Cooper admonished "With all due respect, that's the argument of a five-year-old."

Bernie Sanders – Sanders was nothing like the first populist insurgent from the left to panic the Democratic party establishment—Eugene McCarthy, Jesse Jackson, Gary Hart, and Howard Dean all preceded him, albeit from different angles of disruption and to varying degrees of success—but he came closer than any of them to redefining the party itself. In 2016, in what proved to be a remarkable, if ill-fated (some cling to "rigged") race against Hillary Clinton, Sanders openly challenged the Democratic faithful to choose between the neoliberal wing of the power-brokers so closely aligned with the Clintons (cozy with Wall St., staunchly pro-NAFTA) and the grassroots wing—more visible than ever on the heels of Occupy Wall St.—that preached single-payer healthcare and breaking up the monopolies of the big banks. That Sanders was also, across his 35+ years in politics, rather casual in his self-identification as a socialist (his own preferred description was "democratic socialist") makes his near-toppling of the Clinton juggernaut all the more impressive. Given how central the insider-vs.-outsider dynamic was throughout the entire election, it's probably not surprising that many in the media drew obvious parallels between Bernie and the guy with the red baseball cap. A couple of these were issues-based—both candidates targeted the corporatist imbalance of free trade, both were vocal in their condemnation of costly foreign interventions—while others revolved around the phenomenal fan energy each campaign so diligently nurtured. Even in some states where Sanders was losing primaries to Clinton, he was massively outdrawing her on the stump, speaking to crowds that rivaled Trump's, both in size and adulation. When Sanders graciously conceded the nomination to Clinton at the Democratic Party Convention, there was much talk (and concern among nervous Democrats) that the "Bernie or bust" crowd would drift towards Trump. It's not clear how big, if at all, a factor this was on November 8—common sense suggests that Sanders supporters who didn't vote for Hillary either opted to go third party or stayed home—but in any event, Sanders himself was having none of it. As he told an interviewer on CNN, "We do not need a president whose cornerstone of his campaign is bigotry, is insulting Mexicans and Latinos, and Muslims and women, who does not believe the reality of climate change when virtually every scientist who has studied this issue understands we are at a global crisis. This is not somebody who should become president." Or as Sanders said elsewhere, sizing up Henry Kissinger in his most memorable debate moment: "Not my kind of guy."

Huey Long – Trump at the dawn of the Great Depression. Banks and corporations were the meteoric Governor of Louisiana's primary targets ("They've got a set of Republican waiters on one side and a set of Democratic waiters on the other side, but no matter which set of waiters brings you the dish, the legislative grub is all prepared in the same Wall Street kitchen"), not immigration policy and trade deals, and— almost unheard of in the south at the time—Long didn't race-bait, so the analogy's far from precise. The similarities were there, though: Long was buffoonish, dictatorial, and vengeful, with a fondness for hanging belittling nicknames on his opponents. "Huey was a mudslinger–a genius at invective, and master of abuse. He could make a nickname fast, and he could make it stick," recalls a contemporary of Long's in Ken Burns' documentary *Huey Long*. Among his more colourful appellations: Turkeyhead Walmsley, Whistle Britches Rightor, Shinola Phelps, Feather Duster Ransdell, and Colonel Bow Wow Ewing. "Little Marco" and "Crazy Bernie" feel woefully inadequate by comparison.

Father Charles E. Coughlin / Henry Ford / Charles Lindbergh – Several commentators, grappling with the Trump phenomenon, reached back to the 1930s for clues, and these three iconic, depression-era Americans provided a useful framework. All three first made their mark outside of politics, becoming larger-than-life figures to huge segments of the population. Their personal accomplishments were, as George W. Bush might say, unbelittlable: Ford as the entrepreneur virtually responsible for creating the auto industry as we know it, Lindbergh for his transatlantic aviation exploits, Coughlin for helping transform the radio medium into a tool of political speech. (If that last comes up a little short on the overall scale of human achievement, consider that Coughlin's on-air sermons/tirades brought in upwards of 30 million listeners, extraordinary numbers in the early days of broadcasting.) More pertinent to the topic at hand: each a fierce advocate of a certain brand of America-Firstism that came widely into play during a tumultuous era—and which, in all three cases, spilled over into Fascism. Not mere flirtations with the stuff, either, but frontline advocacy, the root cause of which was hatred of Jews (leavened somewhat with populist-based fears of interventionism and global trade). Though Trump reserved most of his enmity for Muslims, Latinos, and women, anti-Semitism lurked around the edges throughout (from his initial refusal to disavow holocaust denier David Duke to an image he re-tweeted from a neo-Nazi message board of a Star of David surrounded by cash), at least until early November, when he released his final campaign ad connecting various Jewish financiers to the collapse of the world economy—an ad that Josh Marshall of *Talking Points Memo* said was "packed with anti-Semitic dog whistles, anti-Semitic tropes and anti-Semitic vocabulary."

Fittingly, Lindbergh, Ford, and Coughlin were semi-fictionalized in Philip Roth's 2004 novel *The Plot Against America* (not a CNN headline, though it might have been), cued up by the story of Lindbergh's rise to the Presidency in 1940, defeating a caught-off-guard FDR, the then-standard bearer of the Democratic Party. With Ford in his cabinet and Coughlin issuing broadsides on the airwaves, President Lindbergh's first major move is to cozy up to the Nazis by signing a pact not to enter America in the war against Germany. "Your choice is simple," declared the media-savvy candidate in his run-up to the White House. "It's not between Charles A. Lindbergh and Franklin Delano Roosevelt. It's between Lindbergh and war." Roth's book has been dubbed "an alternative version of American history," the only difference with Trump being that he plays out an alternative version of the American present on a minute-by-minute basis.

Hitler / Mussolini – There was no shortage throughout the 2016 campaign of Hitler = Trump and Benito = Donald equations. Sometimes they took the shape of well-reasoned, historically sound exegeses on the subject. In his essay "Trump: The American Fascist," Robert Reich (writing on his blog, robertreich.org) calmly begins by noting, "I've been reluctant to use the 'f' word to describe Donald Trump," then follows through with a staggering number of parallels that seem irrefutable, at least based on the evidence of Trump the campaigner (Reich posted the piece in March 2016). More frequently, however, such equations played out as Facebook memes, often in the form of ridiculous (usually deliberately so) animated gifs. Photos of Trump with his arm raised high were mutated into Seig Heiling Nazi salutes; detailed A-B comparison charts were common (Hitler "thought Jews should wear special IDs"; Trump "thinks Muslims should wear special IDs"); Il Duce became "Il Douche"; many such items parodied the form itself, such as the jpeg declaring the comparison case-closed because Hitler "drank water" and Trump "drinks water." Trump-as-fascist, both as theory and as meme, has been unleashed, it won't go back in the box, and Trump is now stuck with it. Until, we'll hazard a guess, the next election cycle. For if Trump owned this story in 2016, it's worth remembering that there was no shortage of similar comparisons during much of George W. Bush's presidency, and for that matter, during Barack Obama's. It's perhaps one of the strongest indications of all about just how polarized the American electorate has become; comparing one's ideological and/or party opponents to the very worst human beings in history is now "just politics" (did we forget to mention the one about "Hitlery" Clinton?). What differentiates the Trump meme from previous instances is that what was once confined to the fringiest parts of the fringes has now clawed its way toward the centre of American politics, and that it is louder and more abrasive than ever.

Vladimir Putin – As if having Lou Dobbs, Hugh Hewitt, David Duke, Scott Adams (of *Dilbert* fame), and Joe the Plumber on your list of supporters wasn't enough, Trump had to go all international-rogue on us and woo Kim Jong-un (North Korea) and Robert Mugabe (Zimbabwe) as well. Trump's most public displays of authoritarian affection, however, have been reserved for Russia's Vladimir Putin, whose name passed the lips of more Americans in 2016 than ever before. Even Hillary Clinton wizened up to what she waggishly termed a "bromance," while geopolitical strategists of all stripes nervously contemplated the prospect of a U.S. presidency sympathetic towards an oligarch merciless in his abuse of human rights. The genesis of the Trump-Putin relationship, and of Trump's fondness for the man, is murky (too much political-financial shadiness to enumerate in this space with any degree of accuracy), and temperamentally the two might seem worlds apart. Putin is frequently described as methodical and shrewd; Trump, in comparison, is unscripted and blunt. On the other hand, Putin has—perhaps in an attempt to soften his KGB-hardened past—cultivated a more cartoonish profile in recent years, taking to the mic at a public charity event in 2012 to sing Fats Domino's "Blueberry Hill," and appearing in much-circulated news photos in 2009 horseback riding bare-chested. Still, hard to say whether these brazen publicity stunts held any particular sway over Trump, who (in a rare display of making good on his "strongest asset...my temperament") generally played it cool in his pronouncements on the Russian leader, telling Matt Lauer during the September 7th Commander-in-Chief Forum that their special fondness for each other was nothing more than a kind of friendly quid pro quo: "If he says great things about me, I'm going to say great things about him."

"What's great about this country is that America started the tradition where the richest consumers buy essentially the same things as the poorest. You can be watching TV and see Coca-Cola, and you know that the President drinks Coke, Liz Taylor drinks Coke, and just think, you can drink Coke, too. A Coke is a Coke and no amount of money can get you a better Coke than the one the bum on the corner is drinking."
— *The Philosophy of Andy Warhol*, 1975

George Steinbrenner — A huge mahogany desk, a darkened room, and an imperious, bejeweled CEO barking out the two words that every employee dreads: "You're fired!" Whose face did you see behind the desk in that scenario, Donald Trump's or George Steinbrenner's? Long before *The Apprentice* provided Trump with the two-word death sentence he's most associated with, Steinbrenner was burning through New York Yankee managers with a vengeance unprecedented in the history of major-league baseball, hiring and firing no fewer than 19 in the period between 1974-1991 (Billy Martin alone was rehired five times). It certainly seemed like Steinbrenner was the star of his own TV show during that era, the most colourful and unpredictable soap opera of the '70s and '80s. Trump, who changed campaign managers three times in the months leading up to the election, continued to keep his curbside-kicking tradition alive beyond the cancellation of *The Apprentice*, and if you closed your eyes and engaged in a little time-shifting, it often felt like it could have been Steinbrenner (who passed away in 2010) as this year's Republican nominee. The two men certainly thought the world of each other, a mutual admiration movingly expressed when Steinbrenner popped up for a touching Schmoopie moment in *The Apprentice's* first season. Trump: "You're a special guy." Steinbrenner: "You're a special guy."

Morton Downey Jr. / Jerry Springer – Downey and Springer's theatrical (had to be a put-on, right?), chaotic, circus-freak versions of the audience-participation talk show pioneered by Phil Donahue not only provided the model for what came to be known as "Trash TV," they were also a forerunner of sorts to this year's Republican debates, where an unusually large group of would-be presidents crammed themselves onto the stage—with Trump right in the middle as frontrunner and lead provocateur—and tried to out-degrade each other in a race to the bottom. *The Morton Downey Jr. Show*, which debuted in 1987, addressed (if that's the right word) skinheads, flag burning, strippers, nudists in Atlantic City, and other such omens of the apocalypse; Downey shouted down guests as "pablum-puking liberals," a thoughtful sobriquet that would surely earn thumbs-up approval from the guy who dubbed Elizabeth Warren "Pocahontas." *The Jerry Springer Show* was originally launched as a sedate, civic-minded issues show in 1991 (Springer once served a term as Cincinnati's mayor in the late '70s), but with Downey having cleared the way, and feeling pressure from ever-wilder competitors, Springer soon shifted the focus to every permutation of sexual deviancy imaginable (an 1998 episode called "I Married a Horse" was pulled after affiliates balked, human-horse nuptials not having earned the level of public acceptance they enjoy today), with every show culminating in brawling, profane tirades, and profound humiliation for participants and viewers alike. From there it was but a few short steps to *Jersey Shore, Celebrity Rehab with Dr. Drew, The Apprentice*, and Donald Trump assuring Marco Rubio in the middle of a political debate that his penis was just fine, thanks.

Axl Rose – For a time in the late '80s, Guns N' Roses' lead singer was the most talked-about, fretted-about, argued-about, and over-analyzed white rock star on the planet. "I don't like boundaries of any kind," mused Rose at the time; "I don't like being told what I can and what I can't say." With controversies swirling around their cover art (some stores refused to carry Guns N' Roses' first album until its crude artwork was altered), lyrics ("Immigrants and faggots/They make no sense to me" sang Rose in "One in a Million"—no mention of walls or Muslims, though), substance abuse, and various other petulant whims (Rose caused riots when his anger with audience members cut concerts short in Montreal and St. Louis; if only he'd practiced Trump's "Get 'em out of here!" method of crowd control), the band seemed doomed to disintegrate from the moment they arrived. Which they did, eventually, and unless he seriously defies the normal aging curve, we can at least be thankful that Trump's departure from the world stage won't be anywhere near as protracted as Guns N' Roses' quarter-century tease.

Roseanne Barr – When the left-of-Bernie Sanders comedienne told an interviewer in June 2016 that "I think we would be so lucky if Trump won, because then it wouldn't be Hillary," many people were perplexed by what they took as a Trump endorsement. It wasn't, Barr has since clarified, just an expression of her extreme distaste for Clinton. The Trump connection makes sense, though: ever since she first came onto the national stage in the late 1980s (right around the same time as Trump—amazing how many people we're writing about date to that same moment), Barr has found herself in the middle of numerous controversies involving her unfiltered opinions, hyper-confrontational style, and working-class anger (albeit with a strong feminist tilt, not a specialty of Trump's). In 2012 she even ran for president herself, drawing 67,000 votes running on the "Peace and Freedom" ticket: "Both the Democratic and Republican parties are bought and paid for by corporate America and cater to the needs of the highest bidder as opposed to the people they claim to represent. I cannot be bought." Trump may or may not have been paying attention.

Sam Kinison — A volcanic late-'80s mutation of Richard Pryor and Lenny Bruce, Kinison took their societally-directed rage (at racism, at prurient hypocrisy) and transformed it into pure primal scream therapy directed at the women in his life who'd wronged him, and at himself for being such a dupe. Not pleasant, and—like Morton Downey Jr. and Jerry Springer—a gateway to the coming quarter-century of people screaming at each other on the internet. "Every generation has someone who steps outside the norm and offers a voice for the unspeakable attitudes of that time. I represent everything that's supposed to be wrong, everything that's forbidden." Kinison died in 1992 at the age of 38, and he remained dead until 2016 when he ran for president.

Don Rickles / Joan Rivers — The Art of the Insult. Rickles, the original rapid-fire diss machine (and still at it—what does he make of Trump?), tended to temper his race-based putdowns with just-kidding mea culpas attached: "They always use the word 'insult' with me, but I don't hurt anybody. I wouldn't be sitting here if I did. I make fun of everybody and exaggerate all our insecurities." Rivers, especially in the last decade of her life, went for the kill with an unapologetic gusto that was hugely influential and forever drawing opprobrium from the celebrities she mocked. She even liked to Tweet: "Lindsay Lohan said she wouldn't mind being under oath because she thought Oath was a Norwegian ski instructor." It would have been nice to see Rickles' and Rivers' influence properly acknowledged during last year's Republican debates/celebrity roasts: instead of "Lyin' Ted" for his secretly-Canadian nemesis, Trump should have just referred to him as "you hockey puck."

Don King – One of Trump's Bizarro D-List celebrity supporters (Bill Maher: "Republicans proved one thing, they will let anybody speak at their convention—Scott Baio, Anthony Sabato Jr...*Donald Trump?*"), King's promotional genius for turning heavyweight title fights into worldwide events helped push boxing to record purses and new levels of international visibility in the 1970s. (1975's "Thrilla in Manila" between Muhammad Ali and Joe Frazier was seen by an estimated worldwide audience of 700 million.) King was every bit as famous, though, for his spectacular head of hair, sartorial splendour, and effervescent gift of gab—not to mention the fact that virtually every boxer who ever worked with King ended up suing him for fraud. No matter: he usually settled out of court, forged ahead with new promotions and business ventures, and has remained dedicated to selling the terrificness of Don King to this very day. "I transcend earthly bounds. I never cease to amaze myself because I haven't yet found my limits. I am quite ready to accept the limits of what I can do, but every time I feel that way—boom!—God touches me and I do something that's even more stupendous than whatever I've done up to then."

"The train I ride goes to God knows where
I don't know and I don't care"
   - "Train to Nowhere," Savoy Brown (1969)

P.T. Barnum – Donald Trump as the second coming of P.T. Barnum was a media cliché from the minute Trump announced his candidacy. "Barnum 2.0" quipped one website; "P.T. Barnum with bad hair" suggested another. The comparison is no more unfounded than it is damning (Barnum's legacy as a huckster somewhat belies the breadth of his actual accomplishments; at the very least, his 81 years on earth were anything but uneventful), though of course it's imprecise. In rough outline, however, there's much that weds the two men, be it the former's staging of events—most famously, his traveling circuses—on the grandest and gaudiest of scales (cf. Trump's Wrestlemania productions), his much-publicized and controversial parading of "museum freaks" like Tom Thumb and the Feejee Mermaid (cf. Dee Snider and LaToya Jackson on *Celebrity Apprentice*), a number of bestsellers to his name (including *The Art of Money Getting*), his brief life as a would-be developer, plus forays into politics and what he himself termed "profitable philanthropy." Even Trump acknowledged his debt to the Americanest of American showmen; on *Meet the Press* in January 2016, he didn't demur at all when Chuck Todd brought up the comparison, stressing that "We need P.T. Barnum, a little bit, because we have to build up the image of our country."

Steve Forbes – Seizing upon a vacuum in the contest for 1996's Republican nomination—the tentative front-runner was 73-year-old Senate Majority leader Bob Dole, not exactly a favourite of his party's perennially disaffected base—the billionaire scion of media magnate Malcolm Forbes jumped into the race with no elective experience and a single issue: an across-the-board flat tax of 17% for all citizens and corporations. Which was basically Trump's far-fetched candidacy in broad outline—Trump had his across-the-border wall, also very flat—or at least how it was initially perceived. Forbes's pet issue and daunting personal fortune weren't nearly enough to secure the nomination, though, as his political instincts and public persona—he came across like some cross between Mitch McConnell and Elmer Fudd—both proved to be woefully underfunded. "This is the real message to send to the Washington power brokers. Thanks to you they have finally met their match and they're going to get their ultimate comeuppance in the race in the weeks ahead as we the people take back the power."

H. Ross Perot – A billionaire and a true political phenomenon—a real character, Sydney Greenstreet might have said—Perot kicked off his independent run for the presidency in 1992 not on an escalator but on *Larry King Live*: "If you're that serious—you, the people—you register me in 50 states..." A deep-seated antipathy for one of the Bushes (in Perot's case, President George H.W.) seemed to be near the top of his list of reasons for running. At one point in early June, Perot improbably—miraculously—led both Bush and Bill Clinton in the polls, but he became more and more erratic as the summer progressed: dropped out, dropped back in, claimed the Bush campaign was secretly plotting to sabotage his daughter's wedding. While Perot didn't win a single state come election day, he did draw almost 20% of the popular vote, arguably enough to put a Clinton into the White House.

Now well into his 80s, Perot was never heard from during the 2016 election, so we never did find out what he thought of Trump—and sadly, Dana Carvey never jumped in to pinch-hit for him: "Remember when you were at that big dinner, Donald, the one with all them priests and bishops, and you started talkin' about Hillary hating Catholics? That was world-class, absolutely first-rate. I said to myself, now there's a man ready to clean out the barn!"

Howard Hughes / David Puddy (*Seinfeld*) – Among uber-rich American business tycoons whose wealth is only eclipsed by their fame, Hughes belongs to a select group that includes Steve Jobs, Bill Gates, maybe a few others, and Donald Trump. But that's not why we're including him here—we've already covered the money angle. Both Hughes and Puddy (the squinting, monosyllabic mechanic who might have been *Seinfeld's* funniest recurring character—"Looks like an Arby's night") share with Trump an affliction that affects, according to one 2010 survey, almost 40% of adult Americans: germaphobia, more clinically known as "mysophobia." The reclusive Hughes took his fear of germs to such an extreme that he burned his own clothing after wearing it and wore tissue boxes in place of shoes; Puddy wasn't nearly that far gone, but he did wear a medical necklace ("What is this symbol?" "It's a germ...") and could barely contain his disgust over Elaine's ratty old slippers ("they're bacteria traps"). From the moment Trump hit the campaign trail, reports started circulating that he faced a seriously awkward situation: he found the act of shaking hands highly distasteful, which for a politician is tantamount to being a doctor who can't stand the sight of blood. (Trump's revulsion at Megyn Kelly's and Hillary Clinton's biological transactions would seem to confirm his dilemma.) He evidently figured out a way of redirecting his thoughts elsewhere, though, and for the rest of the campaign could be seen pressing the flesh in rope-line after rope-line. Cleans his teeth ten times a day, scrub away, scrub away, scrub away...

"I don't mean words like 'God' and 'mother' and 'President' and 'suicide' and 'meat cleaver.' I mean simple little words like 'if' and 'hope' and 'you.'"
    - Bob Dylan, interview with Nat Hentoff (1966)

Herman Cain – In 2012, a warm-up for the circus of 2016, it was Cain (and Rick Perry) who brought the laughs. The one-time Pizza King (CEO of Godfather's for a decade) jumped into the Republican field with an idea—"9-9-9," his suspiciously pared-down tax plan (and possible tribute to British New Wave)—a disarming and sometimes bizarre spontaneity ("And when they ask me who is the president of Ubeki-beki-beki-beki-stan-stan I'm going to say, you know, I don't know"), and, as with Trump, seemingly no cognizance of the fact that if he were to win the nomination, there'd be a chance he might end up as president one day: "Okay, Libya...President Obama supported the uprising, correct? President Obama called for the removal of Gaddafi. Just wanted to make sure we're talking about the same thing before I say, 'Yes, I agreed. No, I didn't agree.'"

Ron & Rand Paul – The unbridled *Gong Show*-like ritual of the Republican debates made it easy to forget that when Libertarian-identified candidate Ron Paul, running for President in 2012, called out the G.O.P. establishment (more or less; it happened during one of the debates, and it scarcely matters now what specific candidate he was addressing) for their costly, immoral, and un-conservative military interventions abroad, more than half of the studio audience erupted with loud jeers. Fast-forward to 2016, and son Rand's similar message had been co-opted (albeit with the subtlety of a 757) by new insurgent Trump, whose own ridicule of the Republican Party was met with wild applause. What a difference four years makes, though hard to say what proportion of this could be attributed to the message vs. the messenger. In any case, Rand's bid for the Oval Office (early on he was touted in some quarters as a bona fide threat to the Republican establishment) nosedived quickly, with the only reasonable explanation being that coherence, consistency, and volume moderation were simply at odds with the Republican electorate this time around.

Arnold Schwarzenegger / Jesse Ventura – Sometime in 2014, between his earlier presidential overtures and his eventual follow-through in 2015, Donald Trump had looked into the viability of running for governor of New York. Trump viewed the office as a possible pathway to the presidency; it's also very likely that the outsider celebrity governorships of Jesse Ventura (Minnesota, 1999-2003) and Arnold Schwarzenegger (California, 2003-2011) figured into his calculations somewhere. Schwarzenegger and Ventura were both possessed of amorphous political identities that very much anticipated Trump (Schwarzenegger, a Republican, gradually moved towards the centre during his two terms; Ventura held a variety of libertarian positions that often confounded left-right categorization), and both emerged from comic-book worlds where brute force carried the day (Schwarzenegger a body-builder/movie action-hero, Ventura a wrestler; voraciously acquiring real estate falls somewhere in between).

Schwarzenegger lasted two terms, Ventura one (neither sought re-election), with lots of tumult along the way for both, including charges of sexual misconduct levelled at Schwarzenegger towards the end of his second term. Ventura, after years of immersing himself in conspiracy culture, contemplated a presidential run in 2016, and in 2017 Schwarzenegger will take over as host of *Celebrity Apprentice*. Eventually, all roads lead to and away from Donald Trump.

Ronald Reagan – Trump is routinely described—by the media, by that part of the Republican establishment horrified by him—as an affront to everything the sainted 40th President of the United States ever stood for (and indeed, even Trump honored Reagan's durability as the last inviolable icon, while lesser mortals like the Pope, John McCain, and George Will ended up squarely in his crosshairs). But like Trump, Reagan in 1980 was still viewed by the Democratic brain-trust (not to mention many Republicans) as an unelectable extremist, a washed-up Hollywood entertainer who just had to be endured for a few months until he disappeared forever: "That he should be regarded as a serious candidate for President is a shame and embarrassment for the country at large to swallow," Barry Farrell wrote about Reagan's 1976 presidential bid, and four years later Jimmy Carter called the idea of electing his Republican opponent "dangerous and disturbing." To paraphrase George W. Bush, you fool me, you can get fooled again.

access hollywood

(early sightings in the movies,
on tv, and between covers)

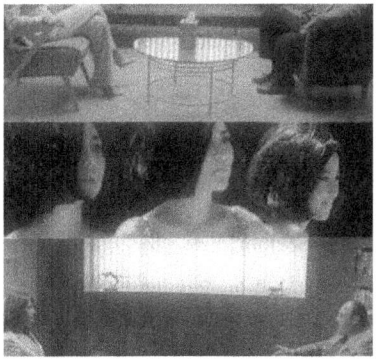

Stephen Colbert – Who knew that when Colbert retired his Comedy Central character in 2014—an extreme-right blowhard who loves only one thing as much as he loves America, namely himself—the mantle would be handily assumed by yet another Republican character who loves to see himself and hear his name on TV, and who has further blurred the line between satire and reality (or between truthiness and a lie)? In 2007, as an adjunct to *The Colbert Report* (and, more significantly, as the blueprint of what was rumoured to be a bid for the 2008 election), Colbert published the *New York Times* bestseller *I Am America (And So Can You!)*, every page of which transports readers, *Back to the Future*-like, into the present. "We need to build a 2000-mile long wall along our southern border. This will have two benefits. First of all, when I'm worried I like to stay busy. Building a giant wall is a great way to keep a nation's mind off how many immigrants enter the country through airports. Second, this wall might actually keep people out. If it's built right, not like that picket fence the Russians threw up across Berlin..."

Lonesome Rhodes (*A Face in the Crowd*, 1957) – As numerous commentators pointed out this election cycle—no Trump movie-connection was made more often—there's a great deal of Trump to be found in Elia Kazan and Budd Schulberg's *A Face in the Crowd*, a feverish mix of such '50s phenomena as Joe McCarthy, television, Madison Avenue, Walter Winchell, and Elvis. Early on, Marcia Jeffries (Patricia Neal)—handler and confidant of Lonesome Rhodes (Andy Griffith), a manipulative jailhouse country-bumpkin savior to the "folks in trouble"— asks Lonesome what it's like "saying anything that comes into your head and being able to sway people like this?" Lonesome, a nastier, more monstrous descendant of Frank

Capra's John Doe, finds such power intoxicating, develops an addiction to it, but complains—manipulatively—that "I just can't get my mouth around some of them things they want me to say." That's okay, another adviser tells him: "telling off presidents and kings" is the way to go, although "You have only one flaw: the way you've suddenly begun to shoot out of control." Rhodes's celebrity gets more and more incandescent no matter what he says, to a point where he announces "I'm not just an entertainer—I'm an influence, a wielder of opinion...a force." It all comes to a spectacular end when Neal surreptitiously triggers the emperor-has-no-clothes moment that many Trump observers had been waiting for since day one—and finally got with the *Access Hollywood* tape, or at least it seemed so at first.

***Bob Roberts* (1992) / J. Billington Bulworth (*Bulworth*, 1998)** – A pair of left-wing, music-heavy satires framing the Bill Clinton era. *Bob Roberts*, directed by and starring Tim Robbins, imagines a folk-singing (Dylan is heavily referenced throughout), arch-conservative populist who wants to repudiate the '60s and make America great again. Playing his Democratic rival for a senate seat, Gore Vidal: "I get vibrations from Mr. Bob Roberts of a very disturbing sort. I haven't any idea who he is. I haven't any idea what he's like. I don't think I'm supposed to have any idea. I know that he proved to be a master of pushing racist buttons and sexist buttons, this and that. The politics of emotion. He's very good at that. What's behind it? I don't see anybody at home." Warren Beatty's *Bulworth* takes aim at both parties—most directly at the welfare-reforming Democratic president then in office—via a bought-and-paid for senator (Beatty) who arranges for his own assassination but decides to say whatever comes into his head on the way out, free-associating the unvarnished truth in incredibly awkward white-guy hip-hop rhyme: "It's hopeless you see/If you're runnin' for office without no TV/If you don't get big money, you get a defeat/Corporations and broadcasters make you dead meat/You been taught in this country there's speech that is free/But free don't get you no spots on TV." As with Trump, the movie sounds like more fun than it actually is.

Bill McKay (*The Candidate*, 1972) – Robert Redford's Kennedy-esque community organizer, the silver-spoon son of a famous father, is a reluctant outsider candidate from the left in Michael Ritchie's *The Candidate*; he views politics as beneath him, but party insider Marvin Lucas (Peter Boyle) convinces him to run for the senate with a promise that he can say and do anything he wants because he has zero chance of winning anyway against incumbent Crocker Jarmon, a political institution. McKay catches on, though, unexpectedly takes over the lead in the polls—getting caught along the way in a push-pull battle with his advisers over simply being himself vs. the need to "pivot"—and wakes up one day to find himself senator-elect. He's supposed to actually govern now, and he hasn't a clue where to begin; "What do we do now?" he famously (and silently) mouths in the direction of Lucas.

Greg Stillson (*The Dead Zone*, 1983) – As portrayed by Martin Sheen, Stephen King's fictional senate candidate—Donald Trump in a hard hat—laces his speeches with a similarly nasty, indignant sense of grievance in David Cronenberg's underrated film adaptation. Stoking Regan-era economic insecurity and silent-majority resentment, Stillson's terrifying destiny is revealed to us and Christopher Walken's Johnny Smith via a psychic handshake. When Smith decides it's his patriotic duty to short-circuit history by exercising his second-amendment rights—shades of Trump's cravenly ambiguous call for gun owners to block Hillary's chance to tilt the Supreme Court—Stillson proceeds to derail his entire political career by grabbing a crying baby as cover. Trump, to be fair, would never do such a thing; he would have already had the baby kicked out.

"Just to check that you're asleep again/President Gas is President Gas again/He comes in from the left sometimes/He comes in from the right."
 - Psychedelic Furs, "President Gas" (1982)

Hal Phillip Walker (*Nashville*, 1975) – Robert Altman's third-party candidate from *Nashville* was the diametric opposite of Trump in at least one respect: Walker is heard but never seen, a disembodied voice emanating from a campaign van, whisked away from the chaotic act that culminates Altman's film like a phantom in the night. But his populist, left-field ideas, appearing at the apex of America's disgust with and distrust of politicians (Vietnam, Watergate), were as flaky as Trump's— get all lawyers out of Washington, change the lyrics to "The Star-Spangled Banner"—and his homespun political wisdom ("When you pay more for an automobile than it cost Columbus to make his first voyage to America, that's politics") just as comically empty. *Nashville* proved to be a harbinger of how the line between politics and entertainment would get progressively blurrier over the next four decades, a line Trump obliterated so savagely and remorselessly during the 2016 primary season that his hapless Republican competitors were left slack-jawed at the starting gate.

***Putney Swope* (1969)** – Robert Downey Sr.'s lampoon of the advertising industry (and racial attitudes, and much else) begins with a board meeting where Putney (Arnold Johnson), the only African-American in the room, is accidentally elected as the new CEO. Putney's path to the boardroom was basically Donald Trump's path to the presidency, especially in the first few Republican debates, when the other 16 candidates gave him close to free rein: "We *all* voted for him—because we thought no one else would vote for him."

Joe Cantwell (*The Best Man*, 1964) – Gore Vidal's Broadway play debuted in 1960, before JFK took office, while Franklin J. Schaffner's film adaptation appeared a few months after his assassination. Vidal's two lead characters took their pedigree elsewhere, though: Cantwell (Cliff Robertson) is Richard Nixon, a ruthless opportunist with a limitless belief in hardball politics, and Henry Fonda's William Russell is Adlai Stevenson, the acerbic and egg-headed (but principled) twice-defeated presidential candidate. It's a little tenuous trying to hang Trump onto Nixon the man (as opposed to Nixon the campaigner): a voracious reader, a student of politics and history, and someone who harbored a lifelong resentment of the privileged class, Nixon was in certain key respects the anti-Trump (not to mention how painfully shy and self-conscious Nixon could be, hardly part of Trump's DNA—both knew how to hold a world-class grudge, we'll give them that). Robertson's bombastic, self-assured, hyper-aggressive Cantwell makes a better match. When Cantwell's campaign manager balks at his latest scheme, Cantwell's snide rejoinder—"Of course you wouldn't—that's why you're a loser and I'm not"—couldn't sound more like Trump. And when Russell takes actions that ensure neither he nor Cantwell will be president, Cantwell is baffled: "You don't understand me...you don't understand politics...you don't understand this country—the way it is, and the way we are." Trump banked the whole way on the very same disconnect.

Fred Van Ackerman (*Advise and Consent*, 1962) – Just like *The Best Man*, *Advise and Consent* both pre- and post-dates JFK in the White House—Alan Drury's novel was published in 1959, Otto Preminger's film ("By far the best political movie ever made in this country" according to Peter Bogdanovich) came along three years later. Essentially a lofty, old-fashioned view of American politics—senators of both parties routinely cross the aisle as their conscience dictates, and even though Senator Seabright Cooley (Charles Laughton) speaks ominously of "evil and powerful men," the senators are mostly honorable people who are mostly trying to do the right thing—George Grizzard's conception of Senator Fred Van Ackerman feels very modern and creepily Trump-like. He's a pariah within his own party, viewed as a pest and a reckless self-promoter (Senator Danta, party whip: "He doesn't belong here, Bob—sooner or later you'll have to cut him off the vine"). The contempt is mutual, as Van Ackerman broods over his exclusion from "the inner-circle, the clique, the club." He's got his own entourage, a subject of great amusement among the older senators. (Danta: "Fred, what do those guys do besides strew roses in your path?" Van Ackerman: "Just my brain trust. You can't hold down a senator's job these days by kissing babies and shaking hands, you know.") He craves media attention, as witness his carefully stage-managed last-minute entrance at a sub-committee hearing while cameras click away (shades of Trump upstaging Cruz at the convention). And when he finds himself cornered, he sweetly hisses out veiled threats: "There are ways to frighten any man, even the senator from Utah." Or, as they say in the Twittersphere, check out sex tape.

Howard Beale (*Network*, 1976) – "I'm mad as hell, and I'm not going to take it anymore," Beale's (Peter Finch) rallying cry from *Network*, has been appropriated by any number of politicians besides Trump. More pertinent is Beale's ratings-mad high-wire act, the idea that an entire nation would compulsively tune into a national newscast to see if this would be the night that the anchor followed through on his promise to commit suicide on-air. Beale's threat was literal; with Trump the high-wire act was metaphorical, but it was the same compulsion that had America obsessing over his every pronouncement for the past year-and-a-half—would today's outrage be the one that killed him off once and for all? "I could stand in the middle of Fifth Avenue and shoot somebody and I wouldn't lose any voters" Trump promised early on, and while his words were tested by several near-death experiences along the way, they proved in the end to be brazenly prophetic.

Guy Grand (*The Magic Christian*, 1969) – The film adaptation of Terry Southern's 1959 novel, in which eccentric billionaire Grand (Peter Sellers) puts to the test his belief that "everyone has their price," is close to unwatchable. (Although Badfinger, who did the soundtrack, ask a question worth pondering: "Will you walk away from a fool and his money?") So we'll hand this one over to Frank Rich, who looked at Trump through the prism of the novel: "In one typical venture, (Grand) pays the actor playing 'an amiable old physician' on a live network medical drama a million bucks to stop in mid-surgery and tell the audience that if he speaks 'one more line of this drivel,' he'll 'vomit right into that incision I've made.' The network,

FCC, and press go into a tizzy until viewers, hoping to see more such outrages, start rewarding the show with record ratings."

Charles Foster Kane (*Citizen Kane*, 1941) – Modelled on William Randolph Hearst, the enigmatic, larger-than-life newspaper magnate from what is allegedly Donald Trump's favourite film (we would have guessed *L'Avventura*) belongs more accurately at the top of a family tree that would include Mark Zuckerberg, Jeff Bezos, and the rest of today's media powerbrokers. But Orson Welles' Kane was also ostentatiously rich, a collector of everything under the sun (including multiple wives), vainglorious and power-crazy, and a man who wanted—expected—the world to bow at his feet. "A toast, Jedediah, to love on my terms. Those are the only terms anybody ever knows—his own." Indeed, Trump's entire campaign at times seemed motivated by nothing more than a single Kane-like proposition: "I think it would be fun to run a country."

The Manchurian Candidate **(1962)** – In J. Hoberman's excellent *The Dream Life*, a rumination on the two-way relationship between American cinema and the American presidency during the 1960s and '70s, Hoberman writes that *The Manchurian Candidate* (part of his "Glamour and Anxiety" cycle of JFK films) "drew attention to the nature of a fantasy regime and the notion of a hidden national narrative." John Frankenheimer's film turns out to be rather adaptable to any post-war president you want to ascribe sinister provenance to—Barack Obama, for one, was widely viewed on the Right as a Manchurian candidate, the Muslim world's "secret agent of history" nurtured into the White House by a subterranean cabal led by Bill Ayers, Saul Alinsky, and the Kenyan Liberation

Army. To view Trump within such a framework isn't that difficult if you accept one of the most popular and mind-bending theories of the 2016 election: that Trump was a mole for the Clintons, hand-picked and encouraged by the Clintons themselves to ensure Hillary's election (and perhaps, from Trump's perspective, to simultaneously annihilate a Republican Party he clearly despised). The origins of the theory trace back to a phone call between Trump and Bill Clinton in the spring of 2015, in which the former president allegedly offered gentle encouragement that Trump join the 2016 Republican field; Trump and the Clintons already had a relationship going back years, involving golf, family weddings, and fundraising, plus Trump had this weird habit of proclaiming "Hillary Clinton is the kindest, bravest, warmest, most wonderful human being I've ever known in my life" every chance he got. The theory faded away, only to return with a vengeance once Trump secured the nomination and seemed intent, via unprecedented weirdness on an almost daily basis through the summer and fall of 2016, on making himself thoroughly unelectable. One serious flaw to the theory is that Laurence Harvey's Raymond Shaw is a haunted, tragic figure, worlds away from Trump's hyperbolic bravado (although Hillary sure made for a fantastic Angela Lansbury). Another is that the thoroughly unelectable candidate won.

Dr. Strangelove **(1964)** – Calling Stanley Kubrick's film a Cold War satire seems woefully reductive. Like *Nashville* or *The Godfather*, it's more like the Rosetta Stone of a half-century of American cinema—look hard enough and you can find whatever you want, even Donald Trump. He's there in Sterling Hayden's General Jack D. Ripper, where conspiracy-fuelled paranoia and germaphobia blur together: "Mandrake, do you realize that in addition to fluoridating water, why, there are studies underway to fluoridate salt, flour, fruit juices, soup, sugar, milk...ice cream. *Ice cream*, Mandrake—children's ice cream." President Muffley (Peter Sellers) and Buck Turgidson (George C. Scott) anticipated a million cable-news panels from this past year as they discussed the ramifications of nuclear Armageddon:

Muffley (horrified Clinton surrogate): "This man is obviously a psychotic."
Turgidson (fair and balanced reporter): "Well, I'd like to hold off judgment on a thing like that, sir, until all the facts are in."

Elsewhere, Turgidson reflects upon America's special love for 2016's two candidates: "It is necessary now to make a choice, to choose between two admittedly regrettable, but nevertheless distinguishable, post-Obama environments." Dr. Strangelove's (Sellers) right arm, the one with a life of its own, is Trump's right arm, no longer Heiling Hitler but instead helplessly Tweeting out bile as his campaign staff frantically tries to beat it back into place. And the pre-credit disclaimer that begins the film became an unanswered prayer that tens of millions of Americans horrified by the thought of President Trump clung to through the final week of the campaign: "It was the stated position of the Founding Fathers that their safeguards would prevent the occurrence of such events as have transpired in this election."

George Patton (*Patton*, 1970) – It's one of the most famous opening shots in film history: with an enormous American flag as a backdrop, the controversial WWII general (played by George C. Scott) addresses his troops, the audience, and an entire country traumatized by Vietnam. "Now, I want you to remember that no bastard ever won a war by dying for his country. He won it by making the other poor dumb bastard die for his country." White House records indicate that Richard Nixon watched *Patton* a dozen times, presumably to strengthen his resolve when making military decisions viewed as criminal by a good part of the American public. Trump may have screened it himself just prior to his Patton-like dismissal of John McCain early in the campaign, an unprecedented ambush that most everyone thought would be enough to sink any Republican after his party's nomination: "He's not a war hero. He was a war hero because he was captured. I like people who weren't captured." When Trump not only survived but flourished in the face of instantaneous condemnation from Jeb Bush ("slanderous"), Lindsey Graham ("disqualifying"), and Marco Rubio ("offensive"), among others, it was clear that from that point forward, no one knew anything anymore.

"The possibility of physical and mental collapse is now very real. No sympathy for the Devil, keep that in mind. Buy the ticket, take the ride."
  - Hunter S. Thompson, *Fear and Loathing on the Campaign Trail '72*

Chauncey Gardiner (*Being There*, 1979) – "In the garden, growth has its seasons. First comes spring and summer, but then we have fall and winter. And then we get spring and summer again." Peter Sellers' beatific, child-like savant in Hal Ashby's *Being There* was a liberal fantasy of the oncoming Reagan decade and the reassuring promises it held out: "security, tranquility, a well-deserved rest." But he was also a post-literate prophecy of Sarah Palin—"I do not read papers; I watch TV"—and, with a foreign policy unapologetically gleaned from Sunday morning political round-tables, of Donald Trump.

Gordon Gekko (*Wall Street*, 1987) – America was given a preview of the 2008 financial meltdown in the late 1980s, a period characterized by insider trading on Wall Street, the proliferation of junk bonds, and the Savings and Loan scandal that cost taxpayers billions. Much as 2008 had its front line of villains and scoundrels—Goldman Sachs, Hank Paulson, Bernie Madoff, George W. Bush—the late '80s had its own rogue's gallery: Charles Keating and Michael Milken, who both served prison time over fraudulent financial practices; "Queen of Mean" Leona Helmsley, a New York hotelier also destined for the big house; and another New York real estate tycoon, Donald J. Trump, who found himself filing Chapter 11 bankruptcy when his Taj Mahal Casino in Atlantic City (financed with junk bonds) faced closure within a year of opening. The whole sordid mess has since become synonymous in the popular imagination with Gordon Gekko, Michael Douglas's reptilian, amoral corporate raider in Oliver Stone's *Wall Street*. Gekko's unapologetic worship of capital is very much in sync with Trump, who spent the entire election hyping how rich he was (far removed from the way shrinking violet Mitt Romney preferred to downplay his wealth) and his inside knowledge of how to game the system ("It's called business," as he so eloquently explained to Hillary during the first debate). Gekko's infamous rumination on greed, meanwhile, offered the clearest glimpse into how Trump (and Forbes, and Perot, and probably most CEO-turned-politicians) viewed the presidency: "The point is, ladies and gentleman, that greed, for lack of a better word, is good. Greed is right, greed works. Greed clarifies, cuts through, and captures the essence of the evolutionary spirit. Greed, in all of its forms:

greed for life, for money, for love, for knowledge, has marked the upward surge of mankind. And greed, you mark my words, will not only save Teldar Paper, but that other malfunctioning corporation called the USA." Nothing to worry about, in other words, or at least nothing I can't fix—it's all just a minor corporation malfunction. (A seemingly irrelevant but nevertheless intriguing real-life twist in this tale came to the surface when Stone revealed, a month prior to the election, that Trump performed a bit part in the 2010 sequel, *Wall Street: Money Never Sleeps*. Stone ended up cutting the scene—"It was too late and too little for where we were, at that point in the movie"—while noting the future President's uncanny confidence: "You know, we did take one with Michael [Douglas] and [Trump] talking in a barbershop. And [Donald] jumped up after the take and he said, 'Wasn't that great?'")

Patrick Bateman (*American Psycho*, 2000) – In Bret Easton Ellis's novel, Bateman—stockbroker by day, chainsaw-crazed serial killer and Huey Lewis fan by night—recommends Trump's *The Art of the Deal* to a detective who's come to interrogate him, with a pull-quote worthy of Trump himself: "It's very good." Mary Harron's film, released almost a decade later, has Bateman (Christian Bale) spotting Trump's car on the streets of Manhattan, and then later Ivana Trump in a restaurant, both times mistakenly ("Why would Ivana be at Texarkana?"). Any deeper connections between Bateman and Trump we'll leave to licensed psychoanalysts, although Bateman's opening monologue is hard to resist: "There is an idea of a Patrick Bateman, some kind of abstraction. But there is no real me—only an entity, something illusory. And though I can hide my cold gaze, and you can shake my hand and feel flesh gripping yours, and maybe you can even sense our lifestyles are probably comparable, I simply...am not...there."

The Joker (*The Dark Knight*, 2008) / Lex Luthor (*Superman*, 1978) – When Christopher Nolan's *The Dark Knight* appeared during the waning months of George W. Bush's presidency, the *Wall Street Journal's* Andrew Klavan picked up on an audacious but unmistakable proposition put forth by the film: Batman was Bush, "vilified and despised for confronting terrorists in the only terms they understand...(pushing) the boundaries of civil rights to deal with an emergency, certain that he will re-establish those boundaries when the emergency is past." Revisited in 2016, one can just as clearly see a side of Donald Trump in Heath Ledger's terrifyingly nihilistic Joker. Was there a better description of Trump in the first few months of the primaries, when he was completely negating every truism ever about what a candidate hoping to win could and could not say, than the Joker's explanation of his own methodology to district attorney Harvey Dent (Aaron Eckhart)? "Do I really look like a guy with a plan? You know what I am? I'm a dog chasing cars. I wouldn't know what to do with one if I caught it. You know, I just...*do things*." If you take a less apocalyptic view of Trump—and hard as it is to say this now, he was very entertaining in those early debates—you can also find him in Gene Hackman's campy portrayal of Lex Luthor in the first blockbuster Superman film. Hackman's Luthor gobbles up desert real estate for self-aggrandizingly nefarious ends (a California that will feature, among other renamed locales, "Marina del Lex"), decks himself out in splashy dinner jackets and a wig, has a sex-bomb girlfriend by his side, and is comically litigious (his first words to Superman: "My attorney will be in touch with you about the damage to the door"). Above all else, Luthor is completely, fully, absolutely in awe of himself: "Doesn't it give you, like, a shudder of electricity to be in the same room with me?"

Biff Tannen (*Back to the Future Part II*, 1989) / Daniel Clamp (*Gremlins 2: The New Batch*, 1990) – In his review of *Gremlins 2* from the *Philadelphia Daily News*, Gary Thompson noted an uncanny appearance in the film by Donald Trump, via a "self-absorbed New York developer" named Daniel Clamp (John Glover). Thompson also remarked that the *Gremlins* sequel was "an unlikely repository of anti-Trump sentiment." No more unlikely, however, than another family entertainment sequel from one year prior, *Back to the Future Part II*, which featured an even more accurately sketched Trump doppelganger in Biff Tannen (Thomas F. Wilson), lifelong arch-nemesis of Marty McFly (Michael J. Fox). That both films satirize/villainize Trump within a year of each other gives you some indication of Trump's stature in popular culture at that particular juncture; still decades away from the universal household name he would later become, Trump was pure New York City tabloid-bait, a shady wheeler-dealer womanizer who knew how to grab a headline. Daniel Clamp's resemblance to Trump hangs mostly on a few loose threads— his name, his wealth, his arrogance, and his spouse Marla— but for the most part the portrait steers clear of actual mimicry. Biff Tannen, on the other hand, is Trump through and through—from the mathematically impossible hair to the boorish insults ("That's right—loser with a capital L!") to his overarching, unselfconscious extravagance. The most chilling bit of ESP regarding the future presidential candidate can be found in the film's opening scene, where an exasperated Biff, after watching Marty and Doc exit the scene in a flying DeLorean, quietly intones, "What the hell is going on here?"

It's a sentiment that has been echoed around the globe millions, if not billions, of times since June 16, 2015.

"The crime you see now, it's hard to even take its measure. It's not that I'm afraid of it. I always knew you had to be willing to die to even do this job. But, I don't want to push my chips forward and go out and meet something I don't understand."
— Ed Tom Bell, *No Country for Old Men* (2007)

Benjamin Horne (*Twin Peaks*, 1990-91) / Noah Cross (*Chinatown*, 1974) – Ruthless and obscenely rich—with much of their fortunes derived from shadowy, predatory, sometimes illegal business dealings—these two business tycoons enjoy secret lives more sinister than we can imagine. Most of the time, they're not very pleasant people: "Sometimes the urge to do bad is nearly overpowering," confesses Horne (Richard Beymer). Superficially after land and property (Horne owns a hotel), they're really after something more profound and elusive: "The future, Mr. Gittes! The future..." Gorgeous daughters: Audrey Horne (Sherilyn Fenn) is part of the family business, and for a time (unbeknownst to Ben) goes undercover at One-Eyed Jacks, her father's secret casino/brothel, which almost leads to Audrey and her father accidentally venturing into some dark place from which Cross (John Huston) and his daughter, Evelyn Mulwray (Faye Dunaway), can never return; Trump...well, we're not going near that one. With the election now over, there will be a million forthcoming explanations of why Trump won. Greil Marcus offered one as early as February 2016: "There are plenty of people who are attracted to Trump, who are secretly thrilled by the current of nihilism he is riding and the spectre of destruction he embodies, but are keeping their mouths shut." Or as Noah Cross put it, "You see, Mr. Gittes, most people never have to face the fact that at the right time and the right place, they're capable of...*anything*."

***Wild Palms* (1993)** – The brainchild of science-fiction novelist Bruce Wagner, this ABC miniseries featured Oliver Stone (still drawing ire over 1991's *JFK*) in the Executive Producer's chair, a strong if not overly familiar cast (save for Angie Dickinson), and the door to a new kind of avant-TV weirdness left ajar by David Lynch's surprise 1990 hit *Twin Peaks*. To no avail: *Wild Palms* tanked. The cult that should have lapped it up once the web hit critical mass just a few years later never materialized, which is too bad; it's some kind of classic paranoia, for sure. Admittedly, to see Donald Trump in *Palms*, you do have to squint your eyes ever so slightly. The first and most obvious place to look is Robert Loggia's Senator Tony Kreutzer, also the mouthpiece for a virtual reality drug he co-invented back in the psychedelic era called Synthiotics (the show is set in the then-future of 2007). A little too manic for Trump and a lot too scientific-poetic (loves to quote T.S. Eliot), Kreutzer nevertheless adores adoration and conveys plenty of self-love regarding the size of his genius to at least semi-qualify. Second, you could turn to Kreutzer's son Coty (Ben Savage). A Synthiotics propagandist at age 11, Coty, not unlike Trumps Eric, Donald Jr., and Ivanka, is clearly being primed by papa as the next generation of family megalomaniacs; episode three of *Palms* is even entitled "Rising Sons." The most intriguing Trump of all, though (keep squinting...), is Dickinson's Josie Ito, who—depending on what side you look at her from—is almost like Donald and Hillary rolled into one package (with a lot of Angela Lansbury in *The Manchurian Candidate* mixed in as well). If the big blonde hair and the 57 face-lifts feel disconcertingly Trump-like, the corporate shilling and temper-flaring feel more ensconced in Clintonland. Whichever direction you look from, Dickinson's Josie is the fictional equivalent of a Donald/Hillary Venn diagram.

David Ferrie (*JFK*, 1991) – Speaking of Stone, Joe Pesci's manic portrayal of drugged-up wack-job David Ferrie comes from some dark corner of American history where secrecy, conspiracy, and big hair intersect. Wearing an orangey-red fright wig rivaled only by Sean Penn's in *Carlito's Way* for garishness, Pesci rants and raves about Castro ("the Beard"), Communism, Oswald, the CIA, and the one "terrible fuckin' weakness" that got him booted out of the seminary. He would have been perfect sitting in for Alex Jones or Sean Hannity one day, maybe even as a Trump stand-in during Hillary's debate prep: "Oh man, why don't you fuckin' stop it? Shit, this is too fuckin' big for you, you know that? Who deleted the e-mails, who forged the birth certificate, fuck man! It's a mystery! It's a mystery wrapped in a riddle inside an enigma! The fuckin' *Drudge Report* don't even know! Don't you get it?"

The Truman Show **(1998)** – It's tempting to view Peter Weir's meditation on reality TV (still relatively new at the time; *The Apprentice* wouldn't debut for another six years) as some crazy pre-enactment of the 2016 Republican nominating contest—Ed Harris's Christof standing in for Roger Ailes, Jim Carrey's Truman Burbank taking the place of Trump—in which a Dr. Frankenstein loses control of his monster and unsuccessfully tries to kill him, but the whole thing takes place inside of a giant bubble anyway, so the monster really has nowhere to go...okay, that's a bit of a reach. Much more pertinent is Harris's opening monologue, his explanation of The Truman/Trump Show's overwhelming pull on its audience: "We've become bored with watching actors give us phony emotions. We're tired of pyrotechnics and special effects. While the world he inhabits is, in some respects, counterfeit, there is nothing fake about Truman himself. No scripts, no cue cards. It isn't always Shakespeare, but it's genuine. It's a life." Notwithstanding, that is, the fact that Trump's advisers spent many agonizing months futilely begging him to stick to the scripts and the cue cards.

Meg Abbott (*The Leftovers*, 2014-15) – When she first appears in season one of HBO's post-apocalyptic drama, Liv Tyler's Meg is in a near-somnambulistic state of depression—a perfect recruit for the Guilty Remnant, a morbid, mysterious cult-like operation whose members smoke as many cigarettes as possible and never speak (their apparent mission is to remind anyone not in the Guilty Remnant of how terrible everything has gotten following the 9/11-type of international crisis the show is based around—not unlike the picture most Republicans have painted of the Obama years). In other words, in terms of temperament and style, Meg is nothing even close to a firebrand like Trump. As season two of the show progresses, however, Meg—mirroring how Trump laid waste to one Republican candidate after another during the primaries—becomes the program's nihilistic centerpiece, determined to perform the unthinkable. "It's pretty fucking amazing, what I'm going to do," she blithely notes, in words which could be lifted from a Trump rally. What her words portend to isn't really clear at that point, but bombing a small town in Texas or perpetrating a mass suicide seem very much within the realm of possibility. That's an altogether different level of damage than what Trump promised, of course, though the shudder of horror both figures evoked in some viewers was similarly palpable.

"...rallying a nation of television viewers to
hysteria, to sweep us up into the White House with
powers that will make martial law seem like
anarchy!"
  - Angela Lansbury as Mrs. Iselin, *The Manchurian
    Candidate*, 1962

Kevin (*Seinfeld*) — The "Bizarro Jerry" only appeared in two episodes during season 8, one of Elaine's new substitute friends for the three who have started to bore her. The two meet at a newsstand where Kevin, overhearing Elaine proclaim that she's not committed to having children, chimes in with his own indifference. Later in the episode, when Elaine lets slip that maybe she does want kids after all, Kevin—after impulsively getting a vasectomy to please his new friend— again concurs: "Sometimes I think I *do* want kids—maybe a lot of kids!" Many commentators took notice that Donald Trump had a similar tendency to base his public statements on whomever he'd spoken to last. Chris Matthews broaches the idea of women being punished for abortions, Trump responds that yes, maybe there should be some punishment; Chris Wallace throws out the possibility of a third-party candidacy, Trump counters that yes, maybe that's something we need to look into. Anderson Cooper: "I've noticed in interviews, and Chris Wallace's interview is another example—maybe it's only on topics where he hasn't thought it through—but [Trump] is highly suggestible." Trump's pliability was most bafflingly on display when, late in the campaign, his daily contortions over immigration seemed to reflect advice coming in from every direction. "Sometimes I think I *do* want illegal immigrants," you kept waiting for him to announce one day, "maybe a lot of illegal immigrants!"

Hank Kingsley (*The Larry Sanders Show*, 1992-98) – Nowhere was what a *Time* magazine cover story dubbed Donald Trump's "Total Meltdown" in the final few weeks of the campaign (accurate at the time, distressingly premature in hindsight) more evident than at the Al Smith Dinner in October 2016, an annual charity event in Manhattan where the two major-party presidential candidates are supposed to step back from the day-to-day partisan rancor and exchange mildly barbed jokes at the expense of both their opponents and (especially) themselves. Obama and McCain participated without a hitch in 2008, as did Obama and Romney in 2012, but Trump's speech that night, with Clinton a few feet away and high officials of the clergy looking on, was met with boos (a little like getting thrown off the set of *Captain Kangaroo*—it just didn't compute) and horrified looks all around. Trump joked about Clinton being too corrupt for the Watergate commission, about possibly pardoning her if elected (or maybe not), and about Clinton pretending not to hate Catholics; having passed through the Don Rickles and Sam Kinison phases of his campaign, Trump had now mutated into Hank Kingsley (Jeffrey Tambor), the hapless sidekick of Gary Shandling's fictional late-night talk show host Larry Sanders. Hank too had a tendency to let loose with the most mortifying attempts to save face whenever cornered or out of his element: in one episode he good-naturedly implied on-air that a substitute bandleader was a child molester (Hank was feeling threatened by the new arrival), and in another, after a joke fell flat, he called out one of the show's writers for being a "retard." Clinton played along and faked laughter throughout Trump's witticisms, except when she didn't; a couple of times the camera caught her shooting icy daggers in Trump's direction, a look of contempt that only needed a disdainfully Hank-like "Hey now!" from her to underscore the many lines that had just been crossed.

Morris Kessler (*Goodfellas*, 1990) – We're betting that Trump, like any self-respecting power-crazed maverick who made his bones in the late-20th century, has seen *Goodfellas* and the first two *Godfathers* numerous times. There must be Trumps all over the place there, right? *The Godfather* films are too dark, too austere, too precisely calibrated to accommodate an outsized personality like Trump—although Moe Greene, staring down Michael Corleone/Rance Priebus in the first *Godfather* and letting him know that he'll be staying in the race, makes for a good fit: "The RNC wants to buy me out? No, I buy you out, you don't buy me out...Do you know who I am? *I'm Donald Trump!*" But *Goodfellas* is Trump to its very core. You can see him in Robert De Niro's Jimmy Conway, working the room and dropping C-notes left and right, and also in Joe Pesci's Tommy DeVito, whose hair-trigger, near-psychotic unpredictability is a force of nature ("He's crazy, he's a cowboy, he's got too much to prove"—Trump's basically Tommy with a Twitter account). Our favourite Trump, though, is the garrulous, bewigged Kessler (Chuck Low), proprietor of Morrie's Wig Shop and accomplice in the airport heist that ends up ripping the Cicero crime family apart: "Morrie? He's a nut job, he talks to everybody. Nobody cares what he says."

Tony Soprano (*The Sopranos*, 1999-2007) – "My ultimate goal is to qualify for helicopter pilot training, afterwards go to work for Trump or somebody, be their personal pilot." So declared Anthony Jr. (Robert Iler), suicidal son of New Jersey crime boss Tony Soprano (James Gandolfini), on the final episode of *The Sopranos*. It's almost too perfect that Trump's name would turn up (twice—later on, Anthony Jr.'s sketchy career goals are chided by his father) in maybe the most celebrated and debated series-ending episode in television history. Points of similarity between Trump and Gandolfini's volcanic, conflicted Mafioso abound, a duality explored by *Vanity Fair*'s Brett Martin in "How Tony Soprano Paved the Way for Donald Trump": the recklessness they shared, the impulsivity, the "body ungoverned by brain." We find the connection a little more tenuous, though: that was one side of Tony, but he was also a study in caution at times, the guy who cleaned up the messes left by others—his crew, his kids, even his enemies—and that's not Trump. (We had a similar problem linking Trump to *Mad Men*'s Don Draper—and we did try.) More revealing, perhaps, is to focus on Tony's relationship with his psychiatrist, Dr. Melfi (Lorraine Bracco), and see it as a version of Trump's relationship with the American electorate. Dr. Melfi is torn: she's fascinated by Tony, at times feels the visceral pull of something new and unpredictable and illicit, and for the most part finds it impossible to cut him loose, however much she's urged to do so by her ex-husband and her own psychiatrist, and however much she knows she's ultimately repulsed by him. Twice, though—at the beginning of Season 5, and again right before the final episode—she does just that, reveals her true feelings and makes a clean break: "You're not a truthful person. You're not respectful of women. You're not really respectful of people...You take what you want from them by force or the threat of force. I couldn't live like that." 47.1% of the American electorate apparently can.

donald is everywhere

(because we are not a collection of
red donalds and blue donalds;
we are the united states of donald)

Andy Warhol – We're referring less to the Campbell's Soup/Marilyn version of Warhol in the '60s—although the idea that in the future, everyone will be president for 15 minutes seems somehow apropos—than to the '70s/'80s version, the well-heeled portraitist who declared in 1975 that "Making money is art and working is art and good business is the best art," then set out to prove it in the years that followed by commissioning lucrative canvasses for the likes of Ronald and Nancy Reagan (not exactly beloved figures among the high art set). All of this was done with typical Warholian flair—if not with tongue firmly in cheek (his worship of money was apparently real) then at least with acute awareness that such gestures would certainly be perceived as ironic. Trump doesn't really do irony, and when he quoted Warhol's "making money is art" aphorism approvingly (in not one but two of his books) there's a good chance he was making a statement, not merely about his ability to make money but about his ability to create great art. And who knows, at least on the terms Warhol laid out, maybe he was on to something. (Or maybe not. For what it's worth, the two attempted an art-business deal of their own in 1981, when Trump commissioned Warhol to paint the Trump Tower. Warhol finished the job, but the deal fell through—Trump didn't like the finished product and never ponied up. Warhol stewed about the slight for years, noting in two separate diary entries from 1984: "I hate the Trumps.")

Camille Paglia – Paglia is here not for her ideas, but instead for the impact with which she once busted through a number of doors marked "sacred," causing various established orders to wince at the mere mention of her name; whatever one feels about Paglia these days, she was inarguably a cultural force for a brief window during the '90s, albeit a force operating on a scale somewhat lesser than making a run for the Oval Office. Residing in the confines of academia for a couple decades, where she honed to a sharp point her various theses (on literature, pop culture, and feminism primarily), she steamrollered into the public eye in 1991 with the release of her provocative 700-page study of art and literature, *Sexual Personae* ("the ability to infuriate both antagonists in an ideological struggle is often the sign of a first-rate book" read one blurb; change the word "book" to "candidate" and you have a readymade Trump encomium too). But it wasn't Paglia's academic credentials that plastered her across every culture-obsessed magazine for the next couple years, it was the verbal hand grenades she set off in interviews and essays, usually lobbed in the direction of second-wave feminism ("I'm going to be as painful as possible until Gloria Steinem screams"), post-modern theory ("it is revolting to see pampered American academics down on their knees kissing French bums"), and Meryl Streep ("she flashes clever accents as a mask for her deeper failures"). Those are Trumpian barbs on so many levels, although, as with Trump, delivery is everything with Paglia. (As an admirer once noted, "she bounces around on the couch like Linda Blair in that scene in *The Exorcist* where all this amazing shit is flying out of her mouth.") For what it's worth, Paglia's politics, like Trump's, have not been easy to track. She expressed deep concern about Trump's unpredictability in an essay for *Salon* this year, but at the same time she viscerally understood part of his appeal: "There's an absurdist, almost Dadaist quality to Trump's candidacy, like Groucho Marx satirizing high society swells in *A Night at the Opera* or the radical Yippies trying to levitate the Pentagon at their 1967 antiwar protest. Trump routinely deploys all the subversive transgressiveness that campus Leftists claim to value. He goes straight as an arrow to the forbidden and repressed."

Marshall McLuhan – Though he's probably best known today for his fourth-wall-shattering cameo in Woody Allen's *Annie Hall*, the Canadian communications theorist (1911-1980) made a number of elliptical pronouncements during his lifetime about the presidency, many of which serve as prescient clues to the political reality show that currently plays out 24/7 on cable news and on the web. From his startling observation following the 1960 JFK-Nixon debate that a "cool" Kennedy trounced a "hot" Nixon for those watching the event on television, while the exact opposite was true on radio, to his declaring on NBC in 1976 (to a mystified Tom Brokaw) that a technical audio mishap was the hands-down winner of a 1976 Ford-Carter debate ("the rebellion of the medium against the bloody message"), McLuhan was never short of a way-out-there soundbite. Whether or not Trump has read McLuhan's 1970 probe (from *Culture Is Our Business*) suggesting that "the politician can no longer 'represent' anybody...he must become his admirers by turning himself into a new image of abstract art," or if he's spent more than 10 seconds even thinking about the man (though for what it's worth, his pal Roger Ailes was pushing *Understanding Media* on Nixon campaign staffers in '68) is irrelevant; what matters is that Trump—the candidate, the meme, the hair, the image pumped into our TV sets intravenous-like—has provided a perfect model on whom students of McLuhan (i.e., anyone who pays even a smidgen of attention to any media anywhere) can hang their own theories and narratives, half-baked or otherwise.

Norman Mailer – The mind boggles surmising what the late novelist and presidential enthusiast would make of the Trump phenomenon. There's a very good chance he would despise the man—for his unfiltered obeisance to his own bank account (Mailer loathed the capitalism-on-steroids direction of modern politics), for his bigotry (true, Mailer was no slouch in that area himself; witness his much-publicized run-ins with feminists and gays, for starters), and maybe more than anything for his anti-intellectualism—the fact that greed and bigotry appear to simply be a part of Trump's makeup, entirely free of self-critique or hand-wringing. On the other hand, Mailer was enthusiastic about Pat Buchanan's 1996 presidential run (well, enthusiastic about certain parts; Mailer believed Buchanan's populist anti-big business message could spark a new right-left alliance), and it's hard to imagine the author of *Advertisements for Myself* not finding at least certain aspects of Trumpism a little tempting. The brash, uber-American-speak finally infiltrating the foreground of Presidential politics (with Trump issuing everything short of a "fuck you!" during the Republican debates), the bloodletting (is there a Democrat in America who hasn't derived some pleasure from Trump's evisceration of certain segments of the G.O.P.?), the comedy, the naming names, the third-person affectation ("Nobody would be tougher on Isis than Donald Trump"), the anti-PC screeds—you know the rest. Mailer himself once took a Donald-type leap into politics, running for Mayor of New York in 1969, with columnist Jimmy Breslin as his running mate. He was defeated soundly at the ballot box (fourth place in a five-person race), but his campaign did leave behind two slogans worth preserving: "No more bullshit" and "Kick the rascals in," at least one of which never made the morning edition of *The New York Times*.

Malcolm McLaren – "Cash from chaos" was the signature slogan of the Sex Pistols' manager/impresario/swindler-in-chief, and it's not hard to locate parallels between the year in British rock 'n' roll owned by the Pistols (1977) and the year in

American politics owned by Donald Trump. Each media-driven shock—the Pistols swearing on national TV or leaving their first record label, E.M.I., with their cash advance in hand; Trump turning hand-size into a fit-for-office criteria or announcing how skilled he'd been as a real estate developer buying off politicians—was followed by another, and then another. To the point where the very notion of a rule book or a code of conduct was smashed to pieces (at least until—as was the case with punk—things more or less returned to normal; it's too early to say what long-term impact Trump will have on Presidential politics or American discourse). McLaren's importance to punk will be squabbled over for decades to come, but his deviously imaginative knack for grabbing a headline and milking it for every shilling is a model few since have mastered, though Trump's instincts in this area have proven to be just as sharp.

Frank Zappa – The thorniest rock and roll star of all-time (revered and reviled in equal measure), Zappa's politics were, depending on who you asked, a model of rational individualism or unspeakable incoherence—not worlds apart (ideologically speaking) from Trump's 30+ years of dabbling across the left-right political spectrum. A self-described "practical conservative" who favoured lower taxes and less government intrusion, Zappa nevertheless was a registered, Dukakis-endorsing Democrat. Long before political correctness was even a thing, Zappa was firmly against it, and yet he apparently had as much use for big-L libertarians as he did for the evangelical wing of the GOP—which is to say pretty much none. An outspoken opponent of authoritarians of all political stripes, Zappa at the same time ruled his own backing bands with something like an iron fist. In the later years of his life, Zappa—whose international admirers included the very un-

Putin-like Vaclav Havel—spoke sincerely about mounting a Presidential bid, stopped in its tracks only by the cancer that took his life. And while there's about as much available evidence that Donald Trump ever read *Spin* magazine as there is that he's read the Bible (Governor Bobby Jindal: "You know that he has not read the Bible because his name is not in the Bible"), you can't help but wonder if he stumbled across this 1991 interview with Zappa while waiting in the doctor's office: "The goal is to run the cheapest campaign in political history. I can sit at home and do talk shows all over the country on radio and answer questions directly to people who might want to vote. And it would cost what? Nothing. I don't believe that you really have to spend fifty million dollars or apply for matching funds from the federal government and then be forced to abide by all those rules in order to do it."

"The day of the man in the white hat or the man on the white horse—or the man who always came to save America at the last moment—someone always came to save America at the last moment—especially in 'B' movies. And when America found itself having a hard time facing the future, they looked for people like John Wayne. But since John Wayne was no longer available, they settled for Ronald Reagan and it has placed us in a situation that we can only look at—like a 'B' movie."
    - "B-Movie," Gil-Scott Heron (1981)

The Book of the SubGenius – At times, it was hard not to entertain the possibility that the entire Trump candidacy was conceived as just one big practical joke—a twisted round of Truth or Dare between Trump and one of his billionaire cronies, perhaps?—and in such a scenario, *The Book of the SubGenius* ("lunatic prophecies for the coming weird times") might have served as Team Trump's operation manual. Published out of Texas in 1983, and revolving around "the sacred teachings of J.R. 'Bob' Dobbs," its pipe-smoking mascot (the actual human perpetrators are Rev. Ivan Stang and Dr. Philo Drummond), *TBOTS* is a cut-and-paste parody of religious cults and political dogma. Rather than dismiss or replace the dogma, though, the SubGenius pranksters blow it up—take it to new levels of apocalyptic absurdity (in the same way that Trump's rhetoric is but an amplified version of Tea Party caterwauling from a few years before). Ideologically neutral, SubGenius doctrine makes a mockery of reasonableness, advocating instead for bullshitting your way through everything ("It is your prerogative to deny your mistakes, or to revel in them—to even pull off your pants and roll in them"), for utilizing "the flexible nature of reality" to tell boldfaced lies (the bolder-faced the better), seeking revenge on enemies ("[The church] is a certified religion of scorn and vengeance directed at THEM"), for communicating with normal people—referred to in the SubGenius lexicon as "pinks"—using hoodoo-voodoo talk ("any inanity spouted by a SubGenius, at any time, automatically becomes part of orthodox, sanctified SubGenius Church Liturgy"), and for making food consumption great again ("Don't just eat that hamburger, eat the HELL out of it!").

The Simpsons ("Bart to the Future," March 19, 2000) – In October 1999, Trump announced on *Larry King Live* that he was forming a Presidential exploratory committee, and, with an initial push from his friend Jesse Ventura, he spent the next few months sort-of but-not-really running to lead the Reform party (on a platform which included the bane of modern Republicanism, a push for universal healthcare). Trump dropped out in February (hardly anybody was aware yet that he was running in the first place), and a month later Fox aired "Bart to the Future." The episode saw Bart peer 30 years ahead in time, only to discover, much to his horror, that he has turned into a hopeless slob (jobless, overweight, turning out sub-sub-standard riffs on his pathetic electric guitar), while sister Lisa is, well, President of the United States of America (the "first straight female President," she clarifies, to the utter befuddlement of anyone who stopped to think about it). When Bart visits Lisa at the Oval Office, she is engaged in a strategy session with her top aides: "As you know, we have inherited quite a budget crunch from President Trump. How bad is it, Secretary Van Helten?" The aide pulls out a graph depicting a sharp 45-degree-angle decline and replies, "We're broke," setting the stage for Bart to clean up his act. It would be another 15 years before Trump appeared on *The Simpsons* again ("Trumptastic Voyage"), though second time around the show's creators were merely satirizing the present, beginning with Homer following the candidate down that dramatic escalator ride in June 2015, fixating on the back of his hair.

Yuge! 30 Years of Doonesbury on Trump – Though Trump has officially run for President just twice, he's floated the idea in at least four separate elections (no doubt many more than that if you happened to be within earshot of him on a regular basis the past three decades), and one steady hand has been tracking this grand folly since September 14, 1987, when G.B. Trudeau's *Doonesbury* strip acerbically mocked a Trump candidacy with an unseen voice emanating from a television: "...and I think most Americans *want* walk-in closets." *Yuge!* is not merely some of the best long-term reportage on the subject, it's a vivid reminder of just how Trumpian Trump the public figure has been all along (so easy was it to get caught up in the weirdness and comedy and ugliness of the campaign, you forget how much actual documented history there is on this guy). The voice—not just the loudness and the awkward syntax but the undiminished self-regard, the amazing ability to steamroll over criticism as if his hearing suddenly went kaput—has been nothing if not consistent.

September 12, 1988: "Ladies and gentlemen, Trump Productions, in association with Donald Trump Promotions..."

November 14, 1999: "As long as I'm a candidate, you have to cover me! Which is good for the Trump brand, which just gets bigger and bigger and bigger."

March 14, 1990: "Marlie Maples is about to become a household name! I guarantee it! It's even rumored that I've got a million dollar bet on it!"

Fittingly, Trudeau's work is heralded on the back cover by Trump himself, with words that could be lifted right out of the preceding pages, if not one of his 2016 press conferences: "I think he's got overrated talent," "A low blow by a sleazeball," "A total loser," and so on.

Donald Trump's Reading List – Though most of the connections we draw in this book are our own, we needn't hypothesize too much about Trump's bookshelf; he provided a "Ten Books I Recommend You Read" list in his 2006 bestseller *Trump 101: The Way to Success*. As with any personal Top 10 list, it provides a few clues about the mindset behind it. First— and utterly surprising to anyone previously unaware that there was gambling going on in Casablanca—is the fact that the first two books listed are written by Donald J. Trump. Second thing to note is that the list is dominated by business and leadership books—ten out of ten, in fact, if you're willing to lump pre-20th century titles by Machiavelli (*The Prince*) and Sun Tzu (*The Art of War*) into a list of "business books" (the latter, anyway, is frequently cited as required reading for would-be CEOs). Beyond that, there are a few interesting tidbits. *Iacocca: An Autobiography* makes sense on a number of levels, from the large-font first-person title to the front cover photo of the auto magnate leaning back in his desk chair (as iconic a rendering of the rags-to-Reagan-'80s as any other image that comes to mind) to the fact that Iacocca himself would later contemplate a bid for the Presidency, going so far as to coin a campaign slogan remarkably Trump-like in its blustery awkwardness: "I Like I." And then there's Norman Vincent Peale's *The Power of Positive Thinking*; published 64 years ago, with millions of copies sold worldwide, the title itself is a catchphrase for the ages, as durable in its way as a Beatles single, and utterly apt for a guy whose most memorable moments of 2016 included calling his opponent a "nasty woman" and professing that she belonged behind bars. Still, for titular prophecy, you can't beat Steven Schragis and Rick Frishman's *10 Clowns Don't Make a Circus: And 249 Other Critical Management Success Strategies*. Change "10" to "17," and in just a few choice words you've summarized as succinctly as possible everything there was to be said about the Republican primaries.

Spy – It's a strange kind of ecosystem for sure, but for a few years during the '80s and '90s, *Spy* magazine and Donald Trump existed in perfectly disharmonious harmony. Trump, the ostentatious, loudmouthed developer was the publication's reason for waking up in the morning, the demon it sought to slay, the most reliable punchline in its bottomless repertoire of barbs. Beginning its run in 1986, the New York-centric magazine was a combination of unflinching satire, celebrity/political gossip, and investigative reporting; its targets were the rich and famous, the powerful and well-connected. Trump more than qualified (his level of fame at that juncture is arguable, though *Spy's* coverage didn't hurt), on top of which he provided the sort of ridiculous soundbite fodder that functions as parody before an editor even lays a hand on it—a character trait that has not diminished in the slightest. Still, it was a coinage from *Spy* co-founder Graydon Carter that received endless replay in the publication and continues (at least according to Carter) to stick to Trump's craw to this day: "short-fingered vulgarian," an even cruder extrapolation of which was hurled at Trump this year by Marco Rubio. In a 2016 interview, former Executive Editor Susan Morrison revealed that Trump, in the first five years of *Spy's* existence, was cited 8.7 times per issue. Some of the more choice Trump features from the period include: "Was Donald Trump Ever Rich?" (a brutal nine-page investigation of his financial transactions, which also lambastes the press for being "pathetically gullible" in all matters re: Trump); "The Art of the Art of the Deal" (Nov. '89, in which a passage from his best-selling book receives an eviscerating line-by-line fact check); and "Nation to Trump: We Need You" (Jan. '88, a presidential prospects scorecard which places Trump, with a walloping 4% support, right between Ricky Schroeder and Joe Biden, though with eerie prescience also notes: "the low-profile noncandidate actually fared increasingly well at decreasing levels of voter income"—if only they'd known).

Twitter – It was a minor big deal in 2008 when Barack Obama deployed Facebook and email blasts to target younger voters (his was the first campaign said to be "web savvy"), but in truth it was mostly a case of conventional methods crammed into a new media template. Certainly, no one older than 14 years old on the receiving end of a "Yours truly, Barack" email had any doubt that this was the work of anyone but a Democratic Party flack—someone from the "messaging" wing of the campaign charged with composing casual-sounding emails in a voice that resembled the candidate's (or Joe's or Michelle's or whoever's). From the get-go (prior to the get-go, actually—@realDonaldTrump began its assault on the nation in March 2009), Trump blew such quaint business out of the water in 140 characters or less, several times a day sometimes, most tellingly while most of America was tucked safely into bed. The difference between the two campaign's approaches is the difference between making use of social media and exploiting it to the hilt (no one can say Trump doesn't relish a good Twitter feud). With its endless profusion of "so SAD!"s and "wow, totally pathetic!"s, and boastful regurgitation of vague and sometimes meaningless poll results—highlighted by its indulgent use of all-caps, exclamation points, and personal insults—no one who has stumbled onto a Trump tweet would mistake for one second that it was anyone but Trump at the other end of the keyboard. To find a similarly effective understanding of communication-through-technology in American political life, you might need to go back eight decades, to Franklin Delano Roosevelt's command of the radio airwaves through his much beloved Fireside chats. With an enormous audience tuned in (as many as 60 million for some broadcasts), FDR formed an intimate bond with listeners, easing their fears about the depression, mobilizing millions by convincing them to continue putting their money in banks, and thus helping to prevent a much-feared national bank run. Trump and his itchy Twitter finger rarely aimed so high—a tweet reminding readers that he "drove Jeb into oblivion" notwithstanding— but his interminable feed riveted many insomniac web surfers with a bent for a certain type of unvarnished performance art. (Or at least until his campaign handlers assumed control of his Twitter account in the waning days of the election, something many insiders—possibly even Melania—wished they had done a year earlier.)

BuzzFeed / TMZ / Gawker – No media outlet suffered for lack of overheated headlines during the most prolonged and vicious election of our lifetime, but perhaps none thrived more in this all-news-all-the-time-even-when-you-don't-actually-want-it environment than these online bastions of click-thru scandal-bait. Trump frequently excoriated the *Washington Post* and *New York Times* throughout the campaign (on the latter, especially, he seems to relish the possibility of their imminent demise—interesting sentiments from someone trying to convince people he has a plan to save American businesses), but in so doing he was merely highlighting—and parlaying to his advantage—the gauntlet against print media that was thrown down years ago by the likes of *TMZ*, *Gawker*, and *BuzzFeed* (and *Reddit*, and *Mashable*, and *BoingBoing*, and...). All three outlets exemplify, in their own way, the new media insatiability critical to Trump's success, and each can lay claim to a specific corner of wall-to-wall insta-coverage (and, to be fair, each of these operations has produced their share of reputable muckraking too; these are not laptop organizations run out of someone's bedroom). *TMZ*, the most popular of the three by dint of the fact that it has branched out into television, is primarily known for its ability to dig below the dirt on some of America's most powerful celebrities; it is all about "the scoop." *Gawker* also specialized in investigative shaming of the rich and famous, but when Hulk Hogan successfully sued them for $140 million in 2016—wrestling, sex tape, lawsuit; you couldn't ask for a more Trump-like maelstrom—they had to close shop for good. The aptly-named *BuzzFeed* delivers "viral digital content" via a splash-page aesthetic which can charitably be described as pop-up advertising in overdrive. It is hardly a startling or bold prediction to suggest that, in the coming Trump epoch, *BuzzFeed* and its ilk will continue to play an ever larger role in the abusive-spouse-like relationship between up-to-the-nanosecond news providers and bleary-eyed surfers.

"I hope it is evident that I do not see the people in the Right Wing as a simple group of fanatics, but rather, as a contradictory stew of reactionaries and individualists, of fascists and libertarians...It could be said that most Right Wingers don't really know what they want. I would not include Mr. Buckley in this category, but I think it can be said the politics of the Right in America reflects an emotion more than an insight."
  – Norman Mailer, "The Debate with William Buckley — The Real Meaning of the Right Wing In America" (1964)

Fox News – For reasons that are primarily aesthetic (moreso than ideological, though that figures in just enough to make the case), Trump's candidacy is hard to fathom without the imprint of Fox News. From its taunting tagline, "fair and balanced," to its lack of volume control and veritable bod-squad of anchorwomen teleported in from the set of *The Stepford Wives*, Fox, like Trump, is more or less designed to get under people's skin. For sheer glitz and overstatement, Trump and Fox would seem to exist as orange and ivory, together in perfect harmony. Not surprisingly, Trump does have close ties with the cable giant, especially with former CEO Roger ("truth is whatever people will believe") Ailes, the person most responsible for steering the network towards the behemoth it is today. Ailes, whose career in the conservative media complex began in 1968 when he was a key consultant on Nixon's presidential campaign, resigned from the network in disgrace in July 2016 following a series of damning sexual harassment allegations, including a lawsuit from popular Fox anchorwoman Gretchen Carlson. Which didn't stop the magnate from reportedly (Trump himself never denied it) advising the candidate on his Presidential debate strategy. An ever more curiouser turn of events, if true, and one that, for months, fed the rumour mill about post-election game plans for each of them, "Trump TV" being the subject of much speculation. (About to happen, by the way, just not exactly as originally envisioned.)

The Drudge Report – The lo-fi collage effect of *The Drudge Report* has long been a striking harbinger of Trump's verbal style on the campaign trail: throw a lot of stuff out there, change it up often, maintain a seemingly disconnected scramble of themes, swat a pesky fly or two while you're at it ("Cops arrest man 'acting like gorilla' and masturbating on sidewalk" intoned one highly memorable *Drudge* link), nail your enemies entirely through inference (Matt Drudge doesn't write stories, he only links to them; Trump doesn't start vicious rumours, he simply retweets what others are already saying). In drawing the arrow from online journalism's original provocateur to Donald Trump, it's helpful to know that a) *The Drudge Report's* hit count first went haywire in 1998 with its breaking of the Monica Lewinsky scandal, and it hasn't let up on the Clintons since; b) Drudge's early support of Trump (the tame term "advocacy journalism" doesn't begin to do justice to how he operates) was blatant enough that even arch-conservative Ted Cruz blasted him during the primary season;

and c) as much as any figure in any medium, Drudge has been a loyal Barack-basher since 2008. But the real connection between candidate Trump and blogger Drudge isn't about content—it's about noise, it's about confusion, it's about blaring sirens.

Glenn Beck – It was something of a shock when Glenn Beck became one of the more prominent names to attach himself to the "Never Trump" coalition that rather clumsily materialized when it became clear Trump was going to win the nomination. It was Beck, after all, who took a back seat to no one in his Obama derangement during the president's two terms—"This president I think has exposed himself over and over again as a guy who has a deep-seated hatred for white people or the white culture...This guy is, I believe, a racist"— using his daily hour at Fox (Beck's show ran from 2009-2011, at which point he was pretty much a media pariah) to spin wild conspiracy theories targeting Van Jones, Anita Dunn, ACORN, and various other people and agencies linked to Obama. Beck's specialty was the elaborate, labyrinthine diagrams he meticulously detailed on the blackboard where much of his show took place, impenetrable enough to put Deputy Andy's cave drawings on *Twin Peaks* to shame. Clearly, Beck had been put on this earth to be a wildly enthusiastic Trump supporter, so his opposition didn't compute—it's almost like he took one look at Trump and decided this was some new kind of crazy that, by way of comparison, might prove to be his own ticket back to the mainstream (and indeed, he started occasionally turning up on CNN this past election cycle for the first time in years).

Joe Wilson – The one constant with Trump this past year was his ability to say things that stopped everyone in their tracks:

"Wow—I've never heard that before." (Too many examples to list—a really early one, now forgotten, was when he told Rand Paul he was ugly in one of the debates.) Before all of that, though, a lot of people said a lot of things during Obama's two terms that cleared the ground for Trump's ever-escalating limits-testing, sometimes in venues and contexts once considered sacrosanct. When Wilson, a South Carolina congressman, twice shouted "You lie!" at the president during a joint session of Congress in 2009 (Obama was trying to pass health care reform at the time), widespread reaction, whether outraged or supportive, pretty much amounted to "Wow— I've never heard that before." Although Wilson didn't support Trump initially—surprising; maybe it was the overpowering lure of one day getting the chance to shout "You're crooked!" at President Hillary Clinton—he came around quickly: "Donald Trump wasn't my first choice, but every time my enthusiasm meter starts to flicker, Hillary says something disgusting and the needle goes back up to maximum."

"Look out honey, 'cause I'm using technology
Ain't got time to make no apology."
   - "Search and Destroy," the Stooges (1973)

Howard Stern / Don Imus – Long-standing enemies—another manifestation of the Groucho Marx rule about not wanting to belong to a club that would have you as a member—these outsized New York radio personalities have spent much of their careers doing battle with that great straw-man of our times, "political correctness" (the practice of which is actually less annoying than people who make a career out of complaining about it). Among Stern's most infamous outrages was his boast that "The closest I came to making love to a black woman was I masturbated to a picture of Aunt Jemima on a pancake box" (thanks for sharing), for which the FCC fined him and his radio station $600,000 in 1992. Imus, meanwhile, caused a firestorm in 2007 when he described the Rutgers University women's basketball team as "nappy-headed hos"—no fine, but a grovelling apology, fleeing advertisers, and a readymade right-wing martyr. Trump has been a friend to both men and frequent on-air guest for decades (his numerous appearances with Stern became the source for a veritable Wikileaks-dump of embarrassing sound clips during the final month of the election), and he was evidently taking notes the whole time: "I think the big problem this country has is being politically correct. I've been challenged by so many people and I don't, frankly, have time for total political correctness. And to be honest with you, this country doesn't have time, either." Partial might not be a bad idea, though.

Bill Maher – Bizarre as it may seem, and as horrified as he might be to admit it, there is a direct line from Bill Maher to Donald Trump. And not just because Maher started hosting ABC's *Politically Incorrect* in 1993, a concept Trump has been dining out on ever since. Much more pertinent as far as this survey goes is the fact that Maher, through both *P.I.* and its HBO follow-up, *Real Time with Bill Maher*, has promoted a stream of outspoken conservative women, all of whom have emerged as Trump surrogates and/or supporters the past year. Chief among them: Ann Coulter (cf. pg. 6), Kellyanne Conway (a Republican pollster who took over as Trump's campaign manager in August 2016, when his numbers were looking particularly grim), Laura Ingraham (talk radio acolyte for Trump), and Monica Crowley (former Nixon intern, also a vocal Trump fan). Some of Maher's critics on the left—and they are plentiful—will never forgive him for letting these women speak, but his own feelings about Trump have been clear for a while. In 2013, at the peak of Trump's Birther campaign, the comedian publicly offered to donate $5 million to charity if Trump provided a copy of his birth certificate proving that he wasn't "spawn of his mother having sex with an orangutan," a joke that earned Maher a $5 million lawsuit from you-know-who. The suit was eventually dropped—whether because Trump knew he couldn't win or because what Maher suggested was true, well, only Trump and his mother know for sure.

Chris Matthews – Though five minutes in front of Fox News might convince you otherwise, it's not like conservative pundits have exclusive rights to televisual bluster. Left of the dial at MSNBC, Matthews (along with fellow shouting heads, past and present, like Keith Olbermann and Lawrence O'Donnell) is liberaldom's reigning noise boy—Chief Interruptus, call him—and if you're of the entirely reasonable (based on decades of evidence) opinion that most of what Trump actually does has very little to do with left-right ideology, Matthews can take at least a tiny bit of credit—though nothing on the order of Hannity and O'Reilly or that ilk—for leading political junkies down into the black hole of the deafening echo chamber known as cable news. Matthews's decibel count is through the roof, his unflappability as an interviewer frequently crosses the line into pushiness (though sometimes to good effect; he's one of the few anchor people on cable news who flustered Trump in 2016, leading the candidate straight into his "women should be punished for abortions" flub), and, despite how overbearing he can be, he has his congenial, crazy-uncle side too—funny, off the cuff, and not at all afraid to embarrass himself, which he does fairly regularly. In short—kind of Trump-like, at least in that awkward, older white guy kind of way.

Morning Joe – For several months early on in the 2016 campaign, MSNBC's *Morning Joe*—with twin hosts Joe Scarborough and Mika Brzezinski, plus stalwart support guy Willie Geist and a rotating cast of pundits and insiders—seemed, more than any other show on cable TV (including, initially, anything on Fox News), to understand the Trump phenomenon, to recognize not just that Trump was in contention, but that there was a good chance he would capture the Republican nomination. While most CNN panels at the time seemed predicated on the assumption that they were witnessing a human Hindenburg, Scarborough and Co. at times could barely contain themselves as they watched in awe while Trump appeared to defy political gravity: brandishing insults that would've destroyed others, turning gaffes into publicity gold. Joe and Mika did not endorse Trump (Scarborough, in fact, often went to great pains to point out that he was a Jeb Bush type of conservative, while Mika, a Democrat, is the daughter of Zbigniew, former National Secretary Advisor to Jimmy Carter), but their extensive Trump coverage was a de facto endorsement of sorts. Well, arguably so. The hosts soon found themselves vilified in several quarters—*Slate*, the *Washington Post*, and *Rolling Stone* all ran condemnations of the program—though perhaps less for the number of hours they spent discussing Trump than for their dewy-eyed approach to the subject. Witness Mika, the day after Trump's speech in Cincinnati on July 6, the one where he couldn't contain his irritation with a buzzing-around mosquito (and which most observers cited as "unhinged"): "You saw him connecting with the crowd in a way that no other politician *in the history of politics* that we know ever could." (Emphasis ours.) And yet, that's just part one in this tale (or maybe part 17; it's a complicated history if you have a few hours to spare with Google). For reasons which have never been entirely clear—if a tipping point occurred it was never widely publicized—the relationship soured, and badly. Trump stopped calling in and even tweeted a vaguely threatening rumour about the hosts, employing his finest Perez Hilton impersonation ("Some day, when things calm down, I'll tell the real story of @JoeNBC and his very insecure long-time girlfriend, @morningmika"); Scarborough pounded his fist even harder on the *Morning Joe* desk with his "this-guy-is-destroying-MY-party" refrain; meanwhile, Mika often seemed on the verge of tears regarding the fate of political discourse in America today. Joe and Mika's palpable anguish would be understandable enough had you never tuned into *Morning Joe* prior to July or August 2016, but to anyone who kept even a casual eye on the show during the 12 months prior, there was an almost *Twilight Zone*-ish tint to their rage.

Larry King / David Letterman – When it came to media strategy, Trump—basically using Newt Gingrich's playbook from 2012—ran circles around the rest of the Republican field: don't bother with quaint artifacts like ads and robo-calls, just rely on the debates and unlimited access to the Sunday-morning roundtables. You don't even need to be invited, simply keep them on speed-dial and call in as it suits you (i.e., every single week). Trump's long-standing mastery of television was perhaps nowhere more evident than his ubiquity on *Larry King Live* and *Late Night with David Letterman* through the 1990s and 2000s. Checking an online log of Letterman's show for his entire CBS run (1993-2015), Trump was on no fewer than 22 times (making for some intriguing pairings: Sarah Silverman, very active in this year's election, followed him in 1998, Anderson Cooper in 2005), and in 2007 his ex-wife Ivana was Letterman's guest. You can only look up transcripts for *Larry King Live* dating back to 2000, but Trump appeared at least 15 times over the next 11 years, including an anniversary show where they switched spots and Trump interviewed King. We don't want to call these two broadcasting giants enablers—we're confident they did not understand the true dimensions of the Pandora's Box they helped open, and by the time it was, after their own shows had called it a day (King caused a brief uproar when he interviewed Trump for Russian television this year), they both seemed a little alarmed. Letterman, speaking to Tom Brokaw in 2016: "At everybody's school you hear, 'The great thing about America is, anybody can grow up to be president.' Oh geez, I guess that might be true."

"Everybody's talkin' bout the stormy weather
What's a man to do but work out whether it's true?"
    - "Teen Age Riot," Sonic Youth (1988)

The McLaughlin Group – There was a bittersweet synchronicity to the death this past summer of John McLaughlin, founder and moderator of the groundbreaking (many would apply a less complimentary adjective) TV show that altered the way people talk to each other about politics on television. Debuting in 1982, McLaughlin and his four panelists ushered in the era of partisan (morphing into hyper-partisan by the 1990s) shouting matches in which each side tries to bulldoze its talking points across by filibustering above the din. As contentious as the presidencies of Bill Clinton, George W. Bush, and Barack Obama were, nowhere was this dynamic more rivetingly and/or nauseatingly on display than in 2016, when CNN gave over three or four hours of programming every night to people yelling at, past, and overtop each other about Donald Trump. It wasn't even always a left-right thing, as two of Trump's fiercest critics, Tara Setmayer and Ana Navarro, were Republicans. Trump's roving band of surrogates/defenders/apologists was led by three mainstays, at least one of whom was usually present on every panel: Kayleigh McEnany, Jeffrey Lord, and Corey Lewandowski. McEnany, a lawyer—and Barbie-dollish blonde enough for Fox—was, if you were sympathetic, a tough, relentless, incredibly loyal Trump advocate, or, if you weren't, the single most annoying person on the planet; other panelists would openly mock, guffaw, and roll their eyes at her more creative spinning. Lord, who worked in the Reagan administration long ago—and therefore was required by blood-oath to lovingly footnote the hallowed Republican icon every other sentence—maintained an engagingly self-deprecating sense of humour about Trump early on in the process, but soon found himself mired in the same kind of convoluted rationalizations as McEnany (the two often left fellow panelists Van Jones and Angela Rye dumbstruck). Lewandowski, Trump's campaign manager until he was dropped in June of 2016 (at which point he moved with disconcerting ease over to CNN as a pundit), felt like a cross between H.R. Haldeman and the bug-eyed father in Twisted Sister's "We're Not Gonna Take It" video. Night after night after night of the three of them explaining What Trump Really Meant when he said such-and-such, as one's own sense of reality gradually became untethered along the way. Exhausting—and it all traced back to John McLaughlin and *The McLaughlin Group*.

Barack Obama – Simple declarative sentence: without Barack Obama, presidential candidate Donald Trump never happens. Besides Trump's intimate connection to the Birther movement cited elsewhere, Obama more generally enraged and discombobulated the Republican Party to such a degree— "Obama Derangement Syndrome," to borrow a term also applied to his predecessors George W. Bush and Bill Clinton; it's a dynamic that looks as if it will henceforth be permanently part of the American political landscape—it seemed almost inevitable in retrospect that the 2016 Republican nominee would be as far away from Obama in temperament, style, and background as humanly possible. Bush, Rubio, Kasich, even Cruz, no matter how closely they did or didn't adhere to entrenched Republican dogma, it became clear early on that this nomination would not be about policy. Simply by virtue of having governed alongside Obama, emerging from the same general universe and speaking the same general language, these men had been irredeemably corrupted in the eyes of angry, disillusioned Republicans. The truest expression of the right's contempt for Obama had to come from some place far beyond politics, beyond governance. The most fanatical Trump supporters weren't looking for anything logical, like legislative gains or philosophical victories. They instead wanted someone who in their eyes couldn't be bought, bullied, reasoned, or negotiated with. They just wanted to watch the world burn.

George Will / Bill Kristol – It's a warning we all hear at an early age, and a lesson that inevitably becomes real sooner or later: be careful what you wish for, you just might get it. For Will and Kristol, two of America's longest-running conservative voices—as columnists, on TV, in government (Kristol worked in the Reagan and Bush Sr. administrations)—Donald Trump presented just such a conundrum, one that proved insurmountable in the end. While both men had eventually thrown their support behind every Republican presidential candidate since Reagan, they often seemed vaguely let down by their party's nominee—pedestrian, essentially moderate next-in-line picks like Bob Dole, John McCain, and Mitt Romney just didn't inspire them, didn't share in Reagan's "bold colors" and sweeping vision. "Has conservatism come so far," Will wondered about Romney in 2012, "surmounting so many obstacles, to settle, at a moment of economic crisis, for this?" Enter Trump four years later, and Will and Kristol (joined, to one degree or another, by Peggy Noonan, David Brooks, Rich Lowry, David Frum, and a number of other guardians of the Reagan myth) found themselves presented with an unmanageable and unimaginable nightmare-version of some of the same qualities they'd been pining for in a nominee. Panic all around: Kristol spearheaded the Never-Trump movement, Will quit the party, Noonan worried a lot. The colors were very, very bold now, believe us—bigly bold.

"You show me Regan's double: same face, same voice, everything. And I'd know it wasn't Regan. I'd know in my gut. And I'm telling you that that thing upstairs isn't my daughter."
     - Chris MacNeil, *The Exorcist* (1973)

Jeb Bush — Caught without a ticket, discovered beneath the truck; a comic needs a straight man, a bully needs a victim, the Joker needs the Batman ("I don't want to kill you! What would I do without you? You...*complete me*"), and Donald Trump needed Jeb Bush—or, as his campaign optimistically tried to sell him, Jeb!, the most superfluous use of an exclamation point since Elaine berated Jake Jarmel on *Seinfeld*. In the first few Republican debates, long before Trump turned on Ted Cruz and Marco Rubio, it was the former Governor of Florida and one-time presumptive favourite for the nomination who was the focus of Trump's invective. The mild-mannered, somewhat wonkish face of the party's establishment wing turned out to be the perfect foil for Trump's kamikaze-like assault: Bush (and, by extension, his brother: "You're pathetic for saying nothing happened during your brother's term when the World Trade Center was attacked and came down") became the embodiment of everything Trump voters loathed about the political class, every bit as culpable as Barack Obama or Hillary Clinton, and Bush's tepid—"low-energy"— defense of himself and his family simply reinforced everything Trump said. When Bush finally struck back in some of the later debates, the train had long since left the station, and on February 20, following another round of resounding primary losses, he officially dropped out of the race: "Despite what you might've heard, ideas matter, policy matters. And I truly hope that these ideas that we've laid out will serve as a blueprint for a generation of conservative leaders." Or as Bobby Jones put it when he tried to process the young Jack Nicklaus: "He plays a game with which I am not familiar."

Mitt Romney – The 2012 Republican nominee inserted himself squarely into this year's election when, speaking at something called the Hinckley Institute in March—one of the more awkward visuals of the campaign—he became the biggest name up to that point to break definitively with Trump: "Let me put it plainly: if we Republicans choose Donald Trump as our nominee, the prospects for a safe and prosperous future are greatly diminished." He also helped spearhead the "Never Trump" effort to maneuver someone else into the nomination, and may even have been angling for the spot himself—it was all so hush-hush and ultimately futile, it was rather hard to tell. In any event, it was four years earlier that Trump's debt to Romney was really struck. The 2012 election was, most Republicans believed—and most indicators seemed to confirm—there for the taking. The economy was still in slow recovery, Obama's approval rating was still consistently below 50%, and the presidency of George W. Bush was, maybe, finally in the rear-view mirror. (There was also an unspoken undercurrent of "Okay, we gave the black guy a chance, now let's move on.") Nominate the right candidate—nominate someone who will first do no harm—and we win. So the big money and, eventually, Republican voters (albeit reluctantly, after an unexpectedly schizophrenic primary season) lined up behind Romney. When he lost—because of a lackluster campaign, because of gaffes (the not-so-private 47% speech), because of demographics, and because he was Mitt Romney—the losing side was stunned, angry, and, in poker parlance, all primed to go full-tilt next time. In 2015, in the early months of the Republican nominating contest, first-do-no-harm was completely off the table, something most political commentators were slow to pick up on.

Paul Ryan – Early on, Ryan made for as perfect a foil for Trump as Jeb Bush: the face of a Republican House that Trump's most fervent supporters despised, the running mate of 2012's equally despised Republican nominee, an unctuous Jimmy Olsen Eagle Scout just biding his time until 2020. (A Ryan video released in April, "Politics These Days," was bizarre at first glance—"What is this for? Ryan's not running for anything right now." As an early marker for 2020, though, the meaning was crystal-clear.) So Trump and Ryan dangled each other on a string for months: Ryan played coy with his endorsement, Trump shrugged his shoulders and did whatever he had to do to make sure he didn't get it (even played a little Hamlet himself with regards to Ryan's own primary challenge), and the mutual animosity and maneuvering between the two was the most intriguing thing going until the conventions. Ryan finally endorsed Trump in early June ("It's no secret that he and I have our differences—I won't pretend otherwise," Ryan basically pretended otherwise), Trump held off for a couple of more months before returning serve, and a business arrangement with all the warmth of the post-divorce relaunch of *The Sonny & Cher Show* in 1976 was struck. Trump's *Access Hollywood* tape once again forced Ryan's hand. "There's an elephant in the room," he announced after disinviting Trump to a big party event in Wisconsin, and then it finally happened, the clean break Trump-haters had been calling for all year: "I'm going to close my eyes and look away from the elephant until the day after the election, and then I will let you know what we're going to do about Donald Trump."

Ted Cruz – Finding the right metaphor for the confluence of events and cast of characters that allowed Donald Trump to win the Republican nomination isn't easy—a perfect storm? chaos theory? the Red Sea parting?—but the biggest gift of all came when the 17-person field was essentially narrowed down to Trump and Texas senator Ted Cruz, the one man who was even more reviled than Trump within the Republican party. It was actually Cruz who, before the voting started (and when Trump was still viewed as an implausible sideshow), seemed to be the most likely renegade outsider to take the nomination, and a win in the Iowa caucuses bolstered his prospects. But Cruz's reputation from his time in the Senate— a grandstanding 21-hour filibuster that embarrassed his colleagues and helped shut down the government, an accusation that his own party's Senate Majority Leader Mitch McConnell had lied, the general queasiness he inspired ("Neurologist Explains Why It's Hard to Look at Ted Cruz's Creepy, Unsettling Face" promised one article circulating online in February 2016)—soon caught up with him, and instead of coalescing around Cruz as the best way to stop Trump, the daunting choice faced by influential Republican voices was instead summed up by Lindsey Graham: "It's like being shot or poisoned—what does it really matter?" For the rest of the campaign Trump and Cruz rolled around in the mud in grand fashion—"Lyin' Ted," tweets and retweets about wives, JFK theories too wild for Oliver Stone—until Cruz finally bowed out in May, after the final humiliation of naming a running mate, Carly Fiorina, at a point where he technically had nothing to run for. Much like Jeb Bush, Cruz was the greatest Margaret Dumont that Donald Trump could have ever asked for. And the way Trump bamboozled Cruz at the convention, using Cruz's non-endorsement speech to set up his grand entrance, was Trump's last inspired act of political theatre for the rest of the election. Outside of winning it, that is.

"The nonsuburban electorate will decide that the system has failed and start looking around for a strongman to vote for—someone willing to assure them that, once he is elected, the smug bureaucrats, tricky lawyers, overpaid bond salesmen, and postmodernist professors will no longer be calling the shots...All the resentment which badly educated Americans feel about having their manners dictated to them by college graduates will find an outlet."
    – Richard Rorty, *Achieving Our Country* (1998)

Nate Silver – Towards the end of the 2012 election, Republicans found a new bête noire to ridicule and get all apoplectic over: the resident statistical guru/editor of the polling website *538*, where Silver had called 99 of 100 states correctly in the last two presidential elections. (He was the specific target of Republican ire; more generally it was math.) Silver, just like in 2008, predicted an easy Obama victory in the waning days of October 2012, completely flying in the face of what many Republicans were convinced was going to be a comfortable win for Romney. The disconnect was so pronounced, some Republican true believer (or a very clever Democratic troll) hastily set up something called "UnSkewedPolls.com," intended to counteract the outrageous liberal bias in polling (Silver was not a pollster himself, but rather an aggregator and analyst of what was already out there). *UnSkewed* had Romney ahead by 7 or 8 points, which turned out be exactly right within a margin of error of +/-15 points...No presidential candidate has ever quoted polls as zealously as Trump did during the first few months of the 2016 primary season, often coming across as a full-fledged *538* geek. "The polls say we're doing very, very well" Trump would promise again and again, and in actual fact (at least until he stopped doing so a month or so into the general, a window that future historians will one day refer to as the pre-rigging phase of the campaign), he was almost always very, very right—righter even than Silver himself this time, who, like most political forecasters, never gave Trump much of a chance to win the nomination. Duly chastened, by election eve he was one of the very few who gave him a decent chance to win the presidency.

The Silent Majority – The striking similarity in tone between the convention speeches of Donald Trump in 2016 and Richard

Nixon in 1968 was picked up by political commentators immediately; like Nixon (and Nixon loyalist Pat Buchanan in 1992), Trump sounded the alarm that Armageddon was close at hand. He also resurrected another Nixon trope during the '68 campaign, the "silent majority"—white, working-class voters, the faceless, stoic backbone of the country (some undetermined subset of which constitute Hillary's basket of deplorables)—enlisted by Nixon and by his VP Spiro Agnew to support Vietnam policies that were greeted with outrage from the left. The concept soon made its way into movies (Peter Boyle's hippie-loathing hard-hat in 1970's *Joe*) and television (Carroll O'Connor as Archie Bunker on *All in the Family*), and also onto the radio (Merle Haggard's "Okie from Muskogee"). "The Silent Majority Stands with Trump" signs started popping up at Trump rallies during the summer, and in his convention speech he reached out to the "the forgotten men and women of our country—people who work hard but no longer have a voice." When Trump started complaining that the press was out to get him, echoing Agnew's immortal characterization of the fifth column as "nattering nabobs of negativism," he was pretty much into the Full Nixon phase of his campaign.

Central Park Five – It was a story that would have gotten a lot more attention in a more normal election, and, unlike much of what we've been dealing with here, one that was truly tragic. In 1989, as five teenagers (four of them African-American and one Hispanic) awaited trial for the rape and murder of a Central Park jogger, real-estate mogul Donald Trump took out a full page in four New York City dailies calling for the return of the death penalty and letting the world know that "I want to hate these muggers and murderers." In retrospect, it was a precise encapsulation of what would become at least three Trump hallmarks during the election of 2016: 1) Act first, (don't) think later—to repeat, *as they awaited trial*; 2) As Alec Baldwin so memorably put it on *Saturday Night Live*, in one of his election-season sketches playing Trump, "The thing about the blacks..."; 3) An utter inability to apologize or admit error—even after the five teenagers had their convictions vacated in 2002 (after someone else stepped forward and confessed), Trump wouldn't budge an inch, not then and not in 2016, when he still insisted the original convictions had been correct: "They admitted they were guilty." The disconnect between such obtuseness and the Trump who predicted "At the end of four years, I guarantee you that I will get over 95 percent of the African-American vote—I promise you" was staggering.

Donald DeFreeze (aka "Cinque Mtume," aka "Field Marshal Cinque") – This is what happens when it's one week till the election, and you're worn out to the point of numbness from 15 months of debates and polls and CNN panels and Trump-Trump-Trump-Trump-Trump-Trump-Trump: you're reading a book about the 1974 kidnapping of Patricia Hearst by the Symbionese Liberation Army, the most infamous American terrorist group of the '70s, and the lines between SLA founder Donald DeFreeze and presidential candidate Donald Trump have blurred beyond recognition. In Jeffrey Toobin's *American Heiress*, an account of the Hearst kidnapping, Toobin describes DeFreeze as media-obsessed, paranoid, given to delusions of grandeur, self-mythologizing, possessed of a persecution complex, and not especially disciplined or strategic—a petty con man swept up by historical currents and making it up on the fly. At a certain point, somewhere that exists at the edge of exhaustion, Trump's October rants about rigging and draining the swamp and lock-her-up even started to sound like distant echoes of the mantra the SLA used to sign off all their communiqués: "Death to the fascist insect that preys upon the life of the people."

Julian Assange – One of the stranger developments during the last few months of the election was the right's awkward embrace of *Wikileaks* founder Assange, the fugitive hacker/whistleblower who has been championed by Noam Chomsky, Michael Moore, Glenn Greenwald, and various other agitators from the left. Assange had promised sensational 11th hour leaks that would fatally damage Hillary Clinton's candidacy and ensure Trump's election; all of a sudden he found himself a welcome guest of Sean Hannity's, with the massive amounts of damaging war-related material Assange had previously leaked from the George W. Bush presidency apparently no longer a problem. In the end, much to the dismay and embarrassment of Trump's more chimerical advisors (Roger Stone: "On Wednesday Hillary Clinton is done"), Assange's October Surprise was put on hold because of "security concerns," the most breathtaking 11th-hour crisis since the wedding of Ross Perot's daughter in 1992. By the time it did surface a few days late (another 2,000 leaked e-mails from Clinton's campaign manager John Podesta, including unseemly Goldman-Sachs speech excerpts from the Democratic nominee), it became little more than a convoluted footnote to the overwhelming Pussy Galore shock value of Trump's *Access Hollywood* video. Assange flitted in and out of the story a little longer, releasing more damning Clinton e-mails, but even before the race was over he was slammed by both Moore and Greenwald, mostly for what had evolved into the blatant politicization of his operation; remarkably, the Mr. Robots at Wikileaks failed to hang a single incriminating bit of evidence on Trump, instead opting to hit 'submit' on their Clinton stash at the damnedest times.

Paris Hilton – When the McCain campaign inserted clips of Paris Hilton and Britney Spears into an attack ad against Obama in 2008 (a hysterically-pitched comment on the "cult of personality" tag which has somewhat dogged the 44th President ever since), some observers cited it as another racially-tinged example of gutter politics. At the very least, it was overreach on McCain's behalf, coming, no less, from a guy who'd made a name for himself outside the corridors of Washington appearing on the late-night talk show circuit. As far as we know, no one has had the questionable sense in 2016 to drag Paris Hilton down to Donald Trump's level, but it's not as though a stronger connection couldn't be drawn. Both are ultra-elite, scandalously wealthy New Yorkers, beloved by gossip columnists everywhere. Both are scions of internationally successful hotelier/developers. Both helped cement their reputations and market share through reality TV—Trump in *The Apprentice*, Hilton in *The Simple Life*, described by the A.V. Club as "a noxious would-be reality comedy that inverts the *Beverly Hillbillies* formula by airlifting grating 'celebutantes' Paris Hilton and Nicole Richie to working-class Arkansas for 28 days of the crazy, surreal survival test that the majority of Americans call everyday life." Sounds like your average presidential campaign, but what makes Hilton and Trump kindred spirits is that the economic disparity between stars/candidates and their viewers/constituents has never been more pronounced. On the other hand, what sets them apart is that Hilton, whatever her merits as a screen presence, was rarely convincing in the role, whereas Trump—to the complete bafflement of his critics—almost always was.

Kanye West – In terms of sheer spectacle, the Trump campaign may not be equalled anytime too soon, but if there's one living, breathing American who could pull it off, it's Kanye. (Indeed, at the 2015 Video Music Awards, the rapper announced his intention to run in 2020; though most of the audience assumed he was joking, he later insisted he was dead serious, and acknowledged he had much homework ahead of him.) Within the various worlds West occupies—hip-hop and pop music, primarily, but also designer fashion, being married to a Kardashian, raising hell on social media—the Kanye Effect is more than just a distant cousin to the Trump Effect, it's more like next of kin. Tweets like a motherfucker ("Maybe I couldn't be skinny and tall but I'll settle for being the greatest artist of all time as a consolation"), never met an awards show he didn't want to crash or a fellow artist or celeb he didn't want to slam, loves to taunt his critics ("*Pitchfork*, the album is a 30 out of 10"), is underrated by everyone but himself insofar as his intelligence is concerned, would no doubt put on a truly terrific—we mean absolutely amazing—show (a Kanye convention would be a sight to behold). Granted, we're unclear about his politics, or which side of the aisle he would likely align himself with (sound familiar?), but back in 2005, during Hurricane Katrina, West did call George W. Bush out on national television for not caring about black people, the nerviest thing anyone said on prime time that year. Responding to a question about whether his 2020 intentions were real, Kanye told *Vanity Fair*, "I hate politics. I'm not a politician at all. I care about the truth and I just care about human beings. I just want everyone to win, that's all I can say, and I think we can."

I know I'm no Olivier,
But if he fought Sugar Ray, he would say
That the thing ain't the ring,
It's the play.
So gimme a stage,
Where this bull here can rage,

And though I can fight, I'd much rather recite
That's entertainment!
  - Jake LaMotta, *Raging Bull* (1980)

***

The Apprentice – Trump's television show is maybe the single most crucial piece of the puzzle in trying to figure out what in the Wide Wide World of Sports just happened. When *The Apprentice* debuted in 2004, Trump's fame was comparatively narrow; he was still largely a New York phenomenon at the time, richer and a bigger celebrity than Larry Bud Melman, but in many other ways a product of the same *Spy*/Letterman Manhattan in-jokiness that the rest of the country just wasn't as preoccupied with. *The Apprentice* exploded Trump's national visibility. Above and beyond that, however, is how the show prepared Trump for winning a nomination very few people gave him even the remotest chance to contest. Anyone who watched that first season—and our commitment to this project is such that one of us can now say he has; seasons 2-14 have been tabled for some other lifetime—would not have been the least bit surprised by what transpired in this year's Republican primaries and debates: just like 12 years ago, the dynamic in 2016 basically amounted to Donald Trump fucking with the heads of 16 Junior Varsity go-getters blindsided by what they'd gotten themselves into. An exchange from *The Apprentice's* second episode:

"I mean, everyone hates you."
"I don't think they hate me."
"Yeah, pretty close."

That was Trump belittling space cadet Sam, but it may just as well have been Ted Cruz or Marco Rubio at the receiving end of such ad hominem attacks. While *The Apprentice* did take time out during every episode for Trump to share some of his art-of-the-deal wisdom ("The big thing in negotiation is to try and figure out your opponent; otherwise you're going to look like an idiot and lose big"—he's looking at you, Jeb Bush), as the first season progressed Trump's insults got bolder and more insidious, to the point where they were the (take your pick) best/worst/only reason to bother watching anymore:

"Nick, I don't know why you think you're such a great
    salesman. Your performance was terrible."
"Who chose this stupid concept?"
"That's one of the worst compliments I've ever heard."
"It was a long, boring explanation, and I didn't wanna hear it."
"Well, we've had some disasters, but this is the worst."
"You've been driving people a little nuts—you know that,
    right?"
"You don't believe in the genetic pool?"

Trump even pounced on his right-hand man George (on loan from Stanley Kubrick's *Eyes Wide Shut*, where he played the gatekeeper) in one of the final episodes for engaging in a little old-guy drooling over Jessica Simpson: "I'm not asking you! What the hell do I have to hear about you for? I don't need to hear your answers!" You simply won't find a more precise distillation of Trump's overarching strategy at last year's Republican debates than those three sentences. *The Apprentice* (celebrity version) is slated to begin its 15th season in January 2017 with a new host, Arnold Schwarzenegger, and presumably a new catch-phrase to end each show: "You won't be back." The U.S.A., meanwhile, will be returning for its 240th season in January, also with a new host.

Miss Universe – In 1996, Donald Trump purchased control of the Miss Universe Pageant for $10 million; for the next two decades, first at CBS and then later at NBC, the yearly event became another part of Trump's ever-expanding (and ever-weirder) business empire. Putting aside how much Trump did or did not personally benefit from the venture—the popularity of the pageants (along with Miss America and Miss Teen America, part of the sale) waxed and waned over the years, and there were also all the inevitable controversies thrown into the mix—it does appear that he internalized some of the ideas put forth by the participants for making the world a better place: "Peace all over the world would be the best deal. And I think I would know how to do it better than anybody else, but peace all over the world." That was Trump talking to the *Portland Press Herald* last August, but it could just as easily have been Miss Rhode Island of 2002 naming the one thing she could have if she could have anything. (We're not trying to be mean—beauty pageant contestants do sometimes talk like that. Donald Trump talks like that a lot.) Trump was forced to sell his interest in Miss Universe in 2015, but the relationship came back with a vengeance during the first debate when Hillary Clinton brought up some disparaging comments Trump had once made about Alicia Machado, a former title holder. For the next week, Hillary's hypothetical 3:00 a.m. phone call from 2008 was transformed into Donald Trump's actual 5:30 a.m. tweet in 2016. Millions of Americans came away from the episode convinced that a good night's sleep was something they wanted from their president. It would seem that just as many concluded "Nah, we're up all night to get lucky."

World Wrestling Entertainment (WWE) – Trump's connections to the world of professional wrestling are well known to fans of the genre (beginning in the late '80s, he has hosted various Wrestlemania events at Trump Plaza, and been one of the sport's biggest boosters), but any attempt to extract meaning from this will necessarily come up short against a YouTube clip entitled "Donald Trump body slams, beats and shaves Vince McMahon at Wrestlemania XXIII." This might be the strangest three-and-half-minutes of Donald Trump's very public life, at least within the context of the fact that he will be steps away from having access to what pundits scarily refer to as the "nuclear codes." The body slam and beating—it's really more of a pummeling—make for a not-ineffective piece of bravura faux-sports acting (we're not suggesting Robert De Niro in *Raging Bull*...), but it's the shave itself that transports the clip into a realm somewhere beyond mere spectacle. "One billionaire is shaving another billionaire's head!" shrieks the announcer, while a gleefully smug Trump humiliates (emasculates?) his rival with an electric razor (you half-expect to see red blood come spurting out of McMahon's skull). It's all a comic book-sized joke, of course, and no one watching would assume otherwise, but if it's not Donald Trump at his most queasily authentic, it does at least provide yet another eye-opening glimpse into how he tactically did away with 16 Republican rivals.

"The movie keeps them off balance to the end. During the first part of the picture, a woman in my row was gleefully assuring her companions, 'It's a comedy. It's a comedy.' After a while, she didn't say anything. Instead of the movie spoof, which tells the audience that it doesn't need to feel or care, that it's all just in fun, that 'we were only kidding,' *Bonnie and Clyde* disrupts us with 'And you thought we were only kidding.'"
   - Pauline Kael, "Bonnie and Clyde" (1967)

Mike Score – If you don't know Mike Score by name, you almost certainly know him by mane. The diagonally obtuse lead vocalist for '80s pop phenom A Flock of Seagulls, Score is the most visible antecedent for Trump's own gravity-defying lid, which does in fact resemble an upside-down (or maybe it's a sideways) seagull, if not necessarily an entire flock of them. Now if only Samuel L. Jackson's *Pulp Fiction* hitman Jules had been one of the 2016 Republican candidates, Trump might have been stopped in his tracks at the first debate: "You, Flock of Seagulls," punctuated by a dismissive gesture in Trump's direction—"You know why we're here?"

"You Can't Always Get What You Want," Rolling Stones – "And he said one word to me, and that was 'dead'..." It's pointless trying to apply a particular motive to Trump's continued use of this 1969 Rolling Stones song as exit music— the closest he had to a signature campaign song—but the oddness of the selection is enough to give pause. Lyrical specificity is rarely a viable option when it comes to matching pop music to political rallies, but as a general rule of thumb, if the idea is that you want to inspire a crowd, you probably want to go out with something that at least conveys a tone of unchecked optimism. A few noteworthy choices of modern presidential campaigns bears out this truism: Fleetwood Mac's "Don't Stop" (Bill Clinton), Boston's "More Than a Feeling" (Mike Huckabee), Abba's "Take a Chance on Me" (John McCain), and Stevie Wonder's "Signed, Sealed, Delivered I'm Yours" (Obama). Whatever lies beneath the surface of any of those, up top at least they are joyous, defiant, happy-days-are-on-the-way songs with lyrical hooks (at least in the choruses) that are simple and sing-alongable. "You Can't Always Get What You Want" is a glorious production, for sure (albeit gloriously wistful, among other things), but its overriding sentiments—things didn't turn out so great after all, did they? let's just cut our losses while we can—are precisely what you don't want to tell your throng, especially when you're positioned as the agent of change and all else that is good in the universe. Bizarre—like so much else about TrumpWorld 2016. We have to assume that either the song was chosen by an asleep-at-the-wheel campaign worker or that Trump grew up, like so many other Americans his age, loving both the Stones and the song (we'll leave the White-House-is-his-personal-Altamont theories to someone more paranoid). And if that's the case, he has a point—"You Can't Always Get What You Want" does still sound great, wherever and whenever: in a puffed-up movie about the Death of the Sixties (*The Big Chill*), for the 14,000th time on local classic rock radio, at a Trump rally. It would have sounded even greater following a Donald Trump concession speech on November 9.

Elvis Presley

"I'm like a stranger
Like a stranger in my hometown,
All them cocksuckers stopped being friendly
But you can't keep a hard prick down."
  – Elvis, "Stranger in My Own Hometown" (1970 outtake)

In August 1977, rock critic Lester Bangs ended his Elvis obituary ("Where Were You When Elvis Died?") with words that have echoed loudly ever since: "...solipsism holds all the cards at present; it is a king whose domain engulfs even Elvis's. But I can guarantee you one thing: we will never again agree on anything as we agreed on Elvis. So I won't bother saying good-bye to his corpse. I will say good-bye to you."

Donald Trump negates Bangs's formulation (or maybe he bolsters it—it's open-ended enough for either interpretation) by flipping it on its head: we will never again disagree on anything as we disagreed on Trump. Or maybe not, because whatever commences with an actual Trump presidency (and we go a little numb trying to formulate what that might entail), one thing is clear from the 15-month period this book covers: several floodgates were opened wide and none of them are likely to be shut anytime too soon. In other words, even in a 2020 campaign sans Donald Trump (far from inconceivable), there will undoubtedly be further expressions of the populist rage he masterfully, recklessly, nihilistically tapped into, more extreme railings against the establishment and the so-called enablers of establishment overlordism (i.e., that nefarious, amorphous entity known as "the media"), and against the battered and bruised language of politics and life itself...not to mention the even grimmer likelihood of continual warfare on the race, gender, religion, etc. fronts. Still, at this particular moment—mere days after an election that seemed to last forever and that was as exhausting for some as it was exhilarating for others (we will never again agree on anything as we agreed on exhaustion)—it is difficult to even imagine a world moving forward in which there is as much focus on and enmity towards a single figure as was the case with Donald Trump in the months leading up to his startling victory.

Which might be the real point of Bangs's words; he's not saying everyone loved or approved of Elvis, not at all—rather, he's suggesting that Elvis was a rallying point to which disparate citizens across many demographic markers (age, gender, race, region) pinned their desires and fears and loves and hatreds. The "agreement," maybe, is simply that he existed and that everyone had something to say about him. We'd argue that Trump, too, is such a figure, and that such figures have been few and far between since the death of Elvis. A short list of Americans who might qualify for having that kind of cultural omnipotence ("monoculture," in one of the clichés of the day) is impressive but short: Michael Jackson? Ronald Reagan? Madonna? Barack Obama?

No doubt, Elvis-as-Trump will strike many as an obscene leap of artistic license, and we don't necessarily disagree; had plausibility, or good taste, been a decisive factor in our methodology, we couldn't have written many of the preceding 100+ entries. (That said, if there isn't already a nightclub act somewhere in America with a pompadour for the ages— maybe even a jokey punk band—named Elvis Trump, there will be by the time this book reaches your hands, rest assured.) Whereas one of these men signalled a new frontier of expansiveness, of crossing musical borders, of delivering good times through art, the other seems to signal a new frontier where higher and more prohibitive borders will be constructed, where public speech may be reduced to epithets and assertions of power, where art itself may seem hopelessly puny in the face of who knows what. But the all-encompassing eat-the-world largesse of both figures ("the reverberations still linger from the shock of his arrival," wrote Peter Guralnick a couple decades after Elvis broke through), the near-religious sway they hold over their respective throngs, can't be brushed aside. Elvis was only 42 when he died, but over just a few short years and through many recordings and performances he enhanced the lives of millions. At age 70, Donald Trump is taking over the scariest job on the planet—in many ways his work is just getting started. Millions of citizens are genuinely hoping he will do as promised and make America great again—whatever that means (presumably, it will be better understood if and when it happens). Just as many citizens, if not more, are simply hoping there is still a presidency to even discuss four years from now. Neither of us, hunkered away in a satellite state known as Canada, professes to have a clue what will happen—we were hoping we'd get to end this by saying good-bye to Trump, but he won't be going anywhere for at least four years. And we won't say goodbye to the corpse of the presidency, because we believe—not necessarily with a great deal of confidence, but again made somewhat easier by a little distance—that the institution will survive just fine. We won't even say good-bye to you—if you took the time to read this book, we probably like you. We'll instead stay right where we are, which is more or less where we started: relaxed and paying attention.

Subjects for Further Research

Where do you stop with a subject like Donald Trump? From the moment we embarked on this project we knew that comprehensiveness was an impossibility, not in the least because more connections kept coming to the fore on a daily basis as the events of the campaign unfolded. Here are some of the more obvious and intriguing proto-Trumps we passed over.

F. Lee Bailey – The one lawyer from O.J. Simpson's legal team who insists, to this day, that O.J. was innocent (cf. Donald Trump and the Central Park Five). From Jeffrey Toobin's *American Heiress* (Bailey was also Patricia Hearst's lawyer): "Bailey's hunger for money dwarfed even his lust for fame and led him into business dealings that might charitably be described as questionable...Then there was the matter of temperament. As a group, trial lawyers abound with self-confidence, but Bailey's belligerent arrogance transcended the norm."

J.R. Ewing (*Dallas*, 1978-1991) – Rich, mean, and—for a few months in 1980—a national obsession.

Nigel Farage – An admission of our shallowness: we bypassed Farage, the most prominent public face of Brexit so we could include instead the other English guy with the funny hair (Boris Johnson). Trump and Farage have made various overtures to each other since November 9, and we suspect it's a relationship we'll continue to hear more about.

***The Great Gatsby* (F. Scott Fitzgerald, 1925)** – "Donald Trump's Gatsbyesque charm" ran a September 2015 headline on CNN.com, and the great romantic anti-hero of American fiction was a frequent point of comparison, though not one which ever connected at our end; maybe more hours on Google will teach you something it didn't teach us.

Kim Kardashian – In an overcrowded field, probably the most famous of all the famous people currently famous primarily for being famous. By no means an open and shut case for predicting Trump, but there's a line of logic running through there somewhere.

Lyndon Larouche – The question isn't why didn't we include an essay on this notorious political insurrectionist (less charitable observers refer to him as a "cultist"), it's when will someone publish an entire book connecting him to Trump? One of the more benignly interesting facts about Larouche is that he currently holds the record for most presidential bids ever—eight in total, seven of them on the Democratic ticket, one from the confines of a jail cell.

It Can't Happen Here **(Sinclair Lewis, 1935)** – No doubt, our most glaring oversight (though the entry on Philip Roth's *The Plot Against America* touches on similar terrain), this widely revisited 1935 novel charts the rise of fascism in America under the leadership of one Buzz Windrip. The book's prophetic title did not put any headline writers out of work in 2016.

National Enquirer / Vice – Two print publications which in many respects foresaw the virtual escapades of many paperless outlets described elsewhere in these tree-based pages (*Drudge*, *BuzzFeed*, et al.). *National Enquirer*'s close ties with Trump have been well documented all year. *Vice* has no ties that we know of but was a harbinger of the anti-PC blitzkrieg that fueled much of Trump's base.

Friedrich Nietzsche – German philosopher who dropped out of the Republican race in the spring of 2016, but not before issuing a stern warning to all but one of his remaining rivals: "Whoever fights monsters should see to it that in the process he does not become a monster. And if you gaze long enough into an abyss, the abyss will gaze back into you."

Pat Paulsen – The sad-sack comedian, known primarily for his support work on *The Smothers Brothers Comedy Hour*, launched several joke presidential campaigns beginning in 1968. His slogan—"Just a common, ordinary, simple savior of America's destiny"—was basically Trump with a little bit of modesty. And while Paulsen never overtly advocated for a wall, he did imply that it wouldn't have been a bad idea back at the very beginning: "All the problems we face in the United States today can be traced to an unenlightened immigration policy on the part of the American Indian."

Rupert Pupkin (*King of Comedy*, 1980) – A little pressed for time, Robert De Niro's 5th-rate stand-up comedian takes a famous talk-show host hostage as a shortcut to glory (cf. Donald Trump and the Republican Party). Improbably, it works. "Why not me? Why not? Stranger things have happened." There are also his hands—as do Trump's, Rupert's hands operate on a wavelength all their own.

"A Nice Place to Visit" (*The Twilight Zone*, 1960) – Cited by many as a clue to Trump's odd campaign promise that Americans will win so much under Trump rule they'll actually get sick of it. In fact, Trump himself noted the episode's influence, at least according to Wayne Barrett's 1992 biography, *Trump: The Deals and the Downfall*.

Charlie Sheen – More winning. We will have so much winning if I get elected that you may get bored with winning. Winning isn't everything, it's the only thing. I love the smell of winning in the morning—it smells like winning. Winning.

Frank Underwood (*House of Cards*, 2013-16) – Supposedly modelled on Frank Cowperwood, protagonist of Theodore Dreiser's *The Financier*—1912, and itself a subject for further research—Underwood for a couple of years looked like America's last word in cynical, power-crazed, amoral politicians: "For those of us climbing to the top of the food chain, there can be no mercy. There is but one rule: hunt or be hunted." Underwood even killed people—not merely shooting them metaphorically out on 5th Avenue, but for real, pushing them in front of subway cars. The machinations that took him into the White House stretched credulity to the breaking point. So: a good dress rehearsal for 2016.

V for Vendetta (2005) – Dystopian nightmares are always a popular place to look if you're trying to scare the bejesus out of yourself imaging the ravages of a Trump presidency (Margaret Atwood's *The Handmaid's Tale* and Ray Bradbury's *Fahrenheit 451* became conversation pieces in 2016 also). "We did what we had to do...Immigrants, Muslims, homosexuals, terrorists. Disease-ridden degenerates. They had to go..."

"It Couldn't Happen Here," Pet Shop Boys (1987) – A worthy, if not in fact superior, update on Sinclair Lewis's horror-fantasy ("now it almost seems incredible"), from an all-time pop duo who will almost certainly grapple with Trump in an interesting way in the years ahead—the only prediction for 2017 we feel even remotely secure about.

Douglas MacArthur – David Halberstam from *The Fifties*: "Like most narcissistic personalities, [MacArthur] idealized life and his role in it: He demanded perfection of himself, and when he erred, he was loath to admit it or accept any responsibility. The blame had to be apportioned—more often than not, to rivals who were suspected of seeking his downfall." In 1951, after MacArthur went completely rogue in Korea, Harry Truman had no choice but to cut him loose. But not before a semi-triumphant homecoming and a memorable farewell address before Congress: "Old soldiers never die; they just tend to start tweeting more and more sporadically."

Many People Are Saying (A Trumpography)

What follows is a reading list that tries to figure out the some of the same things we do. Everything is available online—we don't provide any URLs, but a Google search of the titles will take you where you want to go—and almost all of it is free, although a few things may disappear behind a paywall if you frequent sites such as *The New York Times* often enough (and a few things will undoubtedly disappear period). We've only included pieces that address the politicians, celebrities, and cultural touchstones that lurk behind Trump—there was enough written on Trump this year that anything broader would be madness. Even narrowed down, though, what we've assembled is far from exhaustive; we limited most entries in the book to two or three corresponding entries here, with one or two extra for the most-analyzed Trump antecedents (e.g., *A Face in the Crowd*). Although we include a few pieces from conservative sites and writers (*The National Review* most prominently, where antipathy for Trump was almost as pronounced as anywhere else), most of what we list is left-leaning—it's a very rigged bibliography. You'll also find a few pieces in here advising *against* the very premise of this book, one of which we contemplated stealing for our subtitle: *A Bunch of Lazy Comparisons to Donald Trump We Couldn't Resist*.

We've read maybe 5% of what we've listed. Now that we're finished, we're looking forward to catching up on some of this stuff ourselves.

Abel, Allen: "How Donald Trump Happened" (*Maclean's*, 2016)

Adams, Don: "Trump's Truman Show" (*Save Jersey*, 2016)

Andendall, Patrick: "How W. Bush & Obama Paved Way for Trump: A History of Risky Precedents for Becoming President" (*Stupidparty Math v. Myth*, 2016)

Andrews, Travis: "Kanye West and Donald Trump: Comparing Their Egos Is a Sport and Trump Doesn't 'Get It'" (*The Washington Post*, 2016)

Apprenticegeezer: "Is Donald Trump the Reincarnation of P.T. Barnum?" (*Daily Kos*, 2016)

Bachrach, Judy: "What's Behind Donald Trump's Obsession with Beauty Pageants?" (*Vanity Fair*, 2016)

Balasubramanyam, Rajeev: "Donald Trump, 'American Psycho' Muse" (*Salon*, 2016)

Ball, Molly: Is the Tea Party Responsible for Donald Trump? (*The Atlantic*, 2016)

Barnes, Fred: "Trump and the Ghost of Barry Goldwater" (*The Wall Street Journal*, 2016)

Barone, Michael: "Is There Any Precedent in History for Donald Trump?" (*Real Clear Politics*, 2015)

Baumann, Paul: "Mailer on Trump" (*Commonweal*, 2016)

Beinart, Peter: "The Republican Party's White Strategy" (*The Atlantic*, 2016)

Berger, J.M.: "How White Nationalists Learned to Love Donald Trump" (*Politico*, 2016)

Bernstein, David: "Why Hillary Clinton Should Be Worried About Ross Perot (*Politico*, 2016)

Bilton, Nick: "The Trump Non Sequitur" (*Vanity Fair*, 2016)

Boot, Max: "How the 'Stupid Party' Created Donald Trump" (*The New York Times*, 2016)

Brackman, Harold: "Presidential Politics and Poor Marshall

McLuhan: Is The Medium No Longer the Message?" (*Jewish Journal*, 2016)

Brawell, Sean: "The 1992 Movie That Predicted Trump" (*Mint Press News*, 2016)

Brown, Hal: "PSY-VU: Dr. Strangelove, Gen. Ripper, Donald Trump, Paranoid and Batshit Crazy" (*Daily Kos*, 2016)

Brownstein, Ronald: "Republicans Need to Get Ready for the Trump Aftershock" (*The Atlantic*, 2016)

Bump, Philip: "Donald Trump: The Perfect Candidate for the Reagan Era" (*The Washington Post*, 2015)

Bunch, Sonny: "From Bane to the Joker, the Batman Villains That Best Explain Donald Trump" (*The Washington Post*, 2016)

Bunch, Will: "How Howard Stern Gave Us Donald Trump" (*CNN*, 2016)

Buric, Fedja: "Trump's Not Hitler, He's Mussolini: How GOP Anti-Intellectualism Created a Modern Fascist Movement in America" (*Salon*, 2016)

Canning, Charlotte: "The Novel and Play That Predicted Donald Trump's Rise – And Countered a Swell of Great Depression Demagoguery" (*The Conversation*, 2016)

Carter, Dan: "What Donald Trump Owes George Wallace" (*The New York Times*, 2016)

Cavna, Michael: "How 'Doonesbury' Predicted Donald Trump's Presidential Run 29 Years Ago" (*The Washington Post*, 2016)

Chafkin, Max and Silver, Vernon: "How Julian Assange Turned WikiLeaks Into Trump's Best Friend" (*Bloomberg*, 2016)

Chait, Jonathan: "Donald Trump Hasn't Killed the Tea Party. He Is the Tea Party" (*New York*, 2016)

Chait, Jonathan: "How Hitler's Rise to Power Explains Why Republicans Accept Donald Trump" (*New York*, 2016)

Chu, Arthur: "No, Trump Isn't the Next Hitler: But His Real

Historical Comparison Is Still Scary" (*Salon*, 2016)

Clift, Eleanor: "Pat Buchanan: Donald Trump Stole My Playbook" (*The Daily Beast*, 2016)

Cobb, Jelani: "The Model for Donald Trump's Media Relations Is Joseph McCarthy" (*The New Yorker*, 2016)

Cole, Juan: "Donald 'Dr. Strangelove' Trump and Some of the Times We Almost Had a Nuclear War" (*Informed Comment*, 2016)

Coppage, Jonathan: "Donald Trump Isn't Herman Cain" (*The American Conservative*, 2015)

Coppins, McKay: "How the Haters and Losers Lost" (*Buzzfeed*, 2016)

Corn, David: "How the Republican Elite Created Franken-trump" (*Mother Jones*, 2016)

Cozzalio, Dennis: "Hal Philip Walker, Albuquerque, 'Nashville' and Election 2016" (*Fear of the Velvet Curtain*, 2016)

Crowley, Monica: "How Donald Trump Is Resurrecting the 'Great Silent Majority'" (*The Washington Times*, 2016)

Cuzán, Alfred: "Okay, Trump May Be Machiavellian. But Which Machiavelli?" (*The Washington Post*, 2016)

Darcy, Oliver: "The Man Who Could Have Stopped Donald Trump" (*Business Insider*, 2016)

DeVega, Chauncey: "It's All Just Wrestling to Donald Trump: Everything the GOP Front-Runner Knows About Politics, He Learned from the WWF" (*Salon*, 2016)

Diamond, Michael: "Avoid Lazy Comparisons to Donald Trump" (*Toronto Sun*, 2016)

Dickerson, John: "Donald Trump Isn't Another Ross Perot" (*Slate*, 2015)

Duray, Dan: "Will the Real American Psycho Please Stand Up: Why Donald Trump Was Patrick Bateman's Hero'"

(*Bookforum*, 2015)

Dyer, Joel: "'Being There,' the Remake; Starring Donald Trump" (*Boulder Weekly*, 2016)

Ehrlich, David: "10 Movie Characters 'Inspired' by Donald Trump" (*Rolling Stone*, 2015)

Elliott, Debbie: "Is Donald Trump a Modern-Day George Wallace?" (*NPR*, 2016)

Ellis, John: "Paul Ryan: Donald Trump's Best Friend" (*American Thinker*, 2016)

Feirstein, Bruce: "Trump's War on 'Losers': The Early Years" (*Vanity Fair*, 2016)

Filion, John: "The Canadian Trump" (*Slate*, 2015)

Finnegan, William: "Donald Trump and the 'Amazing' Alex Jones" (*The New Yorker*, 2016)

Fisher, Marc: "The Movie That Foretold the Rise of Donald Trump" (*The Washington Post*, 2016)

Fluss, Harrison: "Donald Trump: American Psycho" (*Jacobin*, 2015)

Foer, Franklin: "Donald Trump Isn't a Manchurian Candidate" (*Slate*, 2016)

Folkenflik, David: "Decades Later, 'Spy' Magazine Founders Continue to Torment Trump" (*NPR*, 2016)

For the Record: "The Blurred Line Between Jerry Springer and Donald Trump" (*USA Today*, 2016)

Foster, Stephen: "Right-Wing Radio Host Regrets That Conservatives Were Turned Into Fact-Free 'Monsters'" (*Addicting Info*, 2016)

Frank, T.A.: "The Sad Fate of Trump's Biggest Losers: Newt, Giuliani, Christie, and Ailes" (*Vanity Fair*, 2016)

Freedland, Jonathan: "The Republicans Created Donald Trump: No Wonder They Can't Stop Him" (*The Guardian*,

2016)

Friedersdorf, Conor: "The Alt-Right Will Rise or Fall with Donald Trump" (*The Atlantic*, 2016)

Friedman, Leonard: "Joe Kennedy: The Precursor to Trump" (*Jewish Journal*, 2016)

Gabler, Neal: "Donald Trump Is the Joker: Forget Mussolini and Hitler, the GOP strongman Is an Authoritarian Populist Straight from Hollywood" (*Salon*, 2016)

Gandelman, Joe: "Did Morton Downey, Jr. Set the Tone for Today's Politics?" (*The Moderate Voice*, 2015)

Gatehouse, Jonathon: "Trumputin: Disturbing Parallels Between Trump and Putin" (*Maclean's*, 2016)

Gee, Marcus: "Why Is Donald Trump So Popular? Look No Further Than Rob Ford" (*The Globe and Mail*, 2015)

Geraghty, Jim: "Donald Trump: Pat Buchanan's Heir" (*National Review*, 2015)

gloriasb: "'Bob Roberts:' The 1992 Movie That Predicted Trump" (*Daily Kos*, 2016)

Goldberg, Jeffrey: "The Hollow Men" (*The Atlantic*, 2016)

Goldberg, Jonah: "How Terror (and Twitter) Could Put Trump in the White House" (*National Review*, 2016)

Goldenberg, Kira: "It's Not the 1930s. But Donald Trump Should Scare Us All the Same" (*The Guardian*, 2016)

Gould, Lewis: "Wendell Willkie: A Forerunner to Donald Trump" (*OUPblog*, 2015)

Graham, David: "The Deep Affinity Between Sarah Palin and Donald Trump" (*The Atlantic*, 2016)

Graham, David: "Would Sun Tzu Endorse Donald Trump's Total-War Political Strategy?" (*The Atlantic*, 2015)

Greenberg, Paul: "Fakes Galore – But Not One of Them Could Match Huey Long" (*Townhall*, 2016)

Guilford, Gwynn: "How the Republican Elite Tried to Fix the

Presidency and Instead Got Donald Trump" (*Quartz*, 2016)

Hanlin, Lesley: "Q: Is 'Huey Long' a Cautionary Tale for the Potential Trump Presidency?" (*Screen Prism*, 2016)

Heffernan, Virginia: "How Howard Stern Owned Donald Trump" (*Politico*, 2016)

Hemphill, Jim: "Bulworth, Beatty, Trump and the Dream of the Political Truth-Teller" (*The Talkhouse*, 2016)

Herman, Douglas: "Before Trump, Sen. Bulworth Spoke Truth to Power" (*Zero Hedge*, 2016)

Herr, Josh: "Why Donald Trump Makes This the Perfect Time to Rewatch 'Network'" (*The Fiscal Times*, 2016)

Hess, Amanda: "How Trump Wins Twitter" (*Slate*, 2016)

Hoadley, Greg: "Rush Limbaugh: Responsible for Donald Trump?" (*Inquisitr*, 2016)

Hoberman, J.: "The Entertainer: Trump l'oeil" (*j. hoberman*, 2016)

Hohmann, James: "Is Trump a Manchurian Candidate? Or Maybe the 1919 Chicago White Sox?" (*The Washington Post*, 2016)

Holden, Charles; Messitte, Zach; and Podair, Jerald: "Donald Trump? Look No Further Than Spiro Agnew" (*Milwaukee Journal Sentinel*, 2016)

Horton, Kaleb: "America May Have Forgotten Schwarzenegger 2003, but Donald Trump 2016 Has Not" (*Vanity Fair*, 2016)

Howard, Adam: "Why Donald Trump and Don King Make Sense Together" (*NBC News*, 2016)

Hufbauer, Benjamin: "How Trump's Favorite Movie Explains Him" (*Politico*, 2016)

Hunt, Arthur: "Donald Trump: Hot Persona for a Cool Medium" (*Second Nature*, 2016)

Hunter, David: "Trump: Maybe Citizen Kane, but Not Lonesome Rhodes" (*American Thinker*, 2016)

Ibish, Hussein: "Warhol's Celebrity Culture Explains Rise of Trump" (*The National*, 2016)

Isenstadt, Alex and Thrush, Glenn: "How Jeb and the GOP Got Trumped" (*Vanity Fair*, 2015)

Jang, Meena and Stone, Natalie: "Donald Trump: 18 Memorable Cameos, From 'Home Alone 2' to 'Sex and the City'" (*The Hollywood Reporter*, 2016)

Johnson, Steve: "Is Donald Trump the Jesse Ventura of National Politics?" (*Chicago Tribune*, 2016)

Kaplan, Alex: "'Morning Joe' Hosts Have Fawned Over Trump Ever Since They Met with Him in September" (*Media Matters*, 2016)

Kendall, Joshua: "Have We Ever Had a President Like Donald Trump?" (*New Republic*, 2016)

Kilkenny, Katie: "A Comprehensive List of All the Times Pop Culture Has Totally Predicted Donald Trump" (*Pacific Standard*, 2016)

Kranish, Michael: "The Inside Story of How 'The Apprentice' Rescued Donald Trump" (*Fortune*, 2016)

Kristof, Nicholas: "The G.O.P. Created Donald Trump" (*The New York Times*, 2016)

Kuhn, David: "Will the Political Establishment Be Trumped by The Donald?" (*National Review*, 2015)

Kurp, Josh: "A 'Simpsons' Episode About Garbage Predicted the Rise of Donald Trump" (*Uproxx*, 2016)

Landry, Peter: "Why Rob Ford Is a Cautionary Tale for Donald Trump's Supporters" (*The Huffington Post*, 2015)

Lasalvia, Jimmy: "Trump and Drudge for the Win, Again: Matt Drudge's Army Is Bigger Than the RNC's" (*Salon*, 2016)

Laslo, Matt: "How Obama Gave Us Donald Trump" (*The

Guardian, 2016)

Lee, Jasmine, and Quealy, Kevin: "The 258 People, Places and Things Donald Trump Has Insulted on Twitter: A Complete List" (*The New York Times*, 2016)

Lemire, Tim: "Mayor Mailer, President Trump" (*Mailer*, 2016)

Leon, Melissa: "The Many Ways Donald Trump Is a Real-Life Lex Luthor" (*The Daily Beast*, 2016)

Lindbergh, Ben: "Lonesome Donald: Revisiting 'A Face in the Crowd' in the Age of Trump" (*The Ringer*, 2016)

Linker, Damon: "How the Republican Noise Machine Created Donald Trump" (*The Week*, 2016)

Lowry, Brian: "Donald Trump's Presidential Candidacy Owes a Debt to Rush Limbaugh" (*Variety*, 2016)

Lowry, Rich: "Our George Wallace" (*National Review*, 2016)

Macdonald, Neil: "Trump Riding the Monster the Republicans Created" (*CBC*, 2016)

Mahler, Jonathan and Flegenheimer, Matt: "What Donald Trump Learned from Joseph McCarthy's Right-Hand Man" (*The New York Times*, 2016)

Marcus, Greil: "A Historical Shudder: Special Election Edition!" (*Pitchfork*, 2016)

Markowicz, Karol: "How Paul Krugman Made Donald Trump Possible" (*The Daily Beast*, 2016)

Martin, Brett: "How Tony Soprano Paved the Way for Donald Trump" (*Vanity Fair*, 2016)

Matthews, Dylan: "The Alt-Right Is More Than Warmed-Over White Supremacy" (*Vox*, 2016)

Mattingly, Phil and Jorgensen, Sarah: "The Gordon Gekko Era: Donald Trump's Lucrative and Controversial Time as an Activist Investor" (*CNN*, 2016)

Mayyasi, Alex: "Henry Ford's Campaign to Make America

Great Again" (*Priceonomics*, 2016)

Merry, Robert: "Donald Trump's Secret Weapon: The Silent Majority?" (*The National Interest*, 2015)

Milbank, Dana: "Donald Trump, America's Modern Mussolini" (*The Washington Post*, 2015)

Milbank, Dana: "Sarah Palin, the Political Mother of Trump" (*The Washington Post*, 2016)

Miller, Stephen Paul: "Is Trump the Manchurian Candidate? Themes in the 1950s Classic Don't Seem So Far-Fetched in 2016 America" (*Salon*, 2016)

Morris, Joanna: "Hard to Tell Donald Trump and Boris Johnson Apart" (*The Northern Echo*, 2016)

Moyers, Bill and Winship, Michael: "A Modern-Day Joseph McCarthy: Donald Trump Is the Latest in a Long Line of American Demagogues" (*Salon*, 2016)

Nessen, Stephen: "4 Ways Donald Trump's Pro Wrestling Experience Is Like His Campaign Today" (*NPR*, 2016)

Nichols, John: "Paul Ryan's Self-Serving Hypocrisy Is Enabling Donald Trump and Ted Cruz" (*The Nation*, 2016)

Oldenburg, Ann: "Don Rickles Rules the 2016 Political Race" (*LifeZette*, 2016)

On Life Things and Thoughts: "What a Young Robert Redford Taught Me About Donald Trump: On the Political Psychology of Election Campaigns" (*onlifethingsandthoughts*, 2016)

Oster, Aaron: "Donald Trump and WWE: How the Road to the White House Began at 'WrestleMania'" (*Rolling Stone*, 2016)

Ostroy, Andy: "The Reason Why Trump Gets Away with Saying Anything He Wants" (*The Huffington Post*, 2015)

Pacific Standard: "The Movie Version of Donald Trump Was

Way More Fun" (*Pacific Standard*, 2016)

Parker, James: "Donald Trump, Sex Pistol" (*The Atlantic*, 2016)

Parton, Heather Digby: "Donald Trump's Spirit Animal Is Tony Soprano: How He Built a Campaign Full of 'Goodfellas Wannabes' (*Salon*, 2015)

Pierce, Charles: "Up in Michigan, Where American Fascism Lived Once Before" (*Esquire*, 2016)

Posnanski, Joe: "Donald Trump and the Fourth Wall" (*JoeBlog*, 2016)

Purdum, Todd: "The Terminator and the Donald" (*Politico*, 2016)

Reisman, Sam: "Pop Culture Warned Us About Trump, Part 4: 'The Dead Zone'" (*The National Memo*, 2015)

Remnick, David: "American Demagogue" (*The New Yorker*, 2016)

Rensin, Mark: "Don't Be Shocked by Donald Trump" (*New Republic*, 2016)

Reynosa, Peter: "Why Comparing Donald Trump to Adolf Hitler Is an Embarrassing Act of Ignorance and Also Political Irresponsibility" (*Huffington Post*, 2016)

Rich, Frank: "Donald Trump Is Saving Our Democracy" (*New York*, 2015)

Rich, Frank: "Ronald Reagan Was Once Donald Trump" (*New York*, 2016)

Rogers, Ed: "Donald Trump Is No Boris Johnson" (*The Washington Post*, 2016)

Rosenwald, Brian: "Donald Trump Isn't Ronald Reagan—He's Barry Goldwater" (*The Daily Beast*, 2016)

Rozzo, Mark: "Was This Robert De Niro Role the Inspiration for Donald Trump's Wild Hand Gestures?" (*Vanity Fair*, 2016)

Schatz, Bryan: "A History of Donald Trump's Bromance with

Vladimir Putin" (*Mother Jones*, 2016)

Scheinman, Ted: "Why Does Camille Paglia Love Donald Trump?" (*Pacific Standard*, 2015)

Schwartz, A. Brad: "Did 'Citizen Kane' Predict Donald Trump?" (*The Daily Beast*, 2016)

Schwartz, Dana: "Donald Trump Has Made Stephen Colbert Great Again" (*Observer*, 2016)

Seaton, David: "Wading In Excrement: Is Donald Trump 'The Magic Christian'?" (*Mint Press News*, 2015)

Sewell, Anne: "'The Dead Zone': Did Stephen King Predict the Rise of Donald Trump?" (*Inquisitr*, 2016)

Shafer, Jack: "Did We Create Trump?" (*Politico*, 2016)

Shafer, Jack: "Donald Trump, American Demagogue" (*Politico*, 2015)

Shephard, Alex: "Donald Trump Is Plagiarizing Richard Nixon's Presidential Campaigns" (*New Republic*, 2016)

Smerconish, Michael: "Right Out of 'Seinfeld,' the Opposite Candidate" (*Philly.com*, 2016)

Smith, David: "From Liberal Beacon to a Prop for Trump: What Has Happened to Wikileaks?" (*The Guardian*, 2016)

Smith, Jamil: "The Central Park Five Ad Told Us Who Donald Trump Really Is" (*MTV*, 2016)

Spencer, Stu and Khachigian, Ken: "Trump Is No Reagan" (*Real Clear Politics*, 2015)

Stanley, Tim: "America's Mirror" (*The Telegraph*, 2016)

Stebenne, David: "Donald Trump Echoes Charles Lindbergh: The History of His Odious Campaign Slogan" (*The Conversation/Salon*, 2016)

Sunderland, Mitchell: "How Ann Coulter Created Donald Trump" (*Vice*, 2016)

Tate, William: "Donald Trump as a Re-imagined Howard

Beale" (*American Thinker*, 2016)

Taylor, Jessica: "Donald Trump's Long Embrace of Vladimir Putin" (*NPR*, 2016)

Thomas, Cal: "Trump Is 'Lonesome Rhodes'" (*The Washington Times*, 2015)

Thomas, Matt: "What I Learned About Donald Trump from Binge-Watching 'The Apprentice'" (*Fusion*, 2016)

Thrasher, Steven: "Rudy Giuliani Is Donald Trump's 'Elder Statesman.' How Fitting" (*The Guardian*, 2016)

Tomasky, Michael: "Look in the Mirror: Fox News Created the Trump Monster" (*The Conversation/Salon*, 2015)

Tracy, Abigail: "Ann Coulter, High Priestess of Trumpism, Takes a Victory Lap" (*Vanity Fair*, 2016)

Troy, Gil: "P.T. Barnum Makes Trump Look Like a Clown" (*The Daily Beast*, 2015)

Tucker, Neely: "Is Jesse Ventura's Unlikely Minnesota Win a Road Map for Donald Trump?" (*The Washington Post*, 2016)

UncommonSense: "Trump Is a Rage Addict and Bannon Is His Chief Enabler" (*Daily Kos*, 2016)

Vognar, Chris: "Did a 60-Year-Old Movie Foreshadow Donald Trump's Rise to Power?" (*The Dallas Morning News*, 2016)

Walsh, Joan: "Mitt Romney Should Be Apologizing for Donald Trump" (*The Nation*, 2016)

Weeks, Linton: "Who Does Donald Trump Remind Us Of?" (*NPR*, 2015)

Wilkinson, Francis: "The Tea Party Meets Its Maker" (*Bloomberg*, 2016)

Wills, Garry: "Disciples of Distrust" (*The New York Review of Books*, 2016)

Wilson, J.: "No, Donald Trump Is Not Like Ronald Reagan or

Ron Paul" (*A Libertarian Future*, 2015)

Wilstein, Matt: "Joe Scarborough Completes His Long Evolution to #NeverTrump" (*The Daily Beast*, 2016)

Wizer, Molly: "Donald Trump: General Patton for President, 2016" (*Red State*, 2015)

Wolcott, James: "How Donald Trump Became America's Insult Comic in Chief" (*Vanity Fair*, 2015)

Zaitchik, Alexander: "At Trump's Coronation, Alex Jones Is King" (*New Republic*, 2016)

Zakaria, Fareed: "How the GOP's Dishonesty Led to the Rise of Donald Trump and Ted Cruz" (*The Washington Post*, 2016)

Zakarin, Jordan: "The 1975 Classic 'Nashville' Predicted Donald Trump and This Crazy Election" (*Yahoo*, 2016)

Zaretsky, Robert: "The Hands of a Leader: Donald Trump and Niccolò Machiavelli" (*Los Angeles Review of Books*, 2016)

Zelitch, Simone: "How Philip Roth Predicted the Rise of Donald Trump" (*Forward*, 2016)

Acknowledgements

Scott – Couldn't have done this without the support and patience of my wife, Jacqueline Baines, and our children, Ava and Elliott; they were there for me even when the reverse was anything but true. What have I done to deserve them?

I might never have never taken this on in the first place (certainly would never have reached the finish line) without Phil Dellio's steady encouragement and unwavering enthusiasm. The words 'fun' and 'writing' long ago ceased to co-exist in the same sentence for me, but this project was different, and my friend/co-conspirator had more than a little to do with that.

A number of people have inspired me in recent years to think harder about politics and movies and music, etc. Chris Buck can bend my ear about Presidential politics (and challenge my most cherished liberal assumptions) for hours at a time anytime he likes. David Newfeld (a great friend for 30 years) and Bob Dobbs (Maui chapter) got me to places with Trump I never would have gotten to on my own—though not, I suspect, as far as they would have liked me to go (regardless of the result, I'm grateful for the indoctrination). It has been a pleasure working on the Greil Marcus website (GreilMarcus.net) since 2014, having front row access to the work of one of my favourite critics. Chuck Eddy, Alfred Soto, Vic Perry, Jeff Pike, and Michael Gonzales deserve thanks for engaging me with sharp writing and lively chatter. On the local front, Gary Robertson and Lori Brendel are people I can turn to, and do

My parents, Stuart and Eileen, encouraged an early interest in electoral politics, while my siblings—plus many members of their own families—have kept the conversation going; eternally grateful to Paul, Joanne, and Valerie.

Phil – This is the third book Scott Woods and I have co-authored. The idea for this one was 100% Scott's, and above and beyond 15 months of endless back-and-forth as we (to quote the subject at hand) tried to figure out what in the hell was going on, it was Scott who kept the whole project together through a few critical weeks towards the end, even though he probably didn't realize it (and would never take credit for doing so even if he did).

Let me now compartmentalize and alphabetize.

Thanks to the usual first-ballot, small-hall group of longtime friends: Norm Ibuki, John Karolidis, Steve Keslick, Tim Powis, Peter Stephens, and Cam Victor. Whatever I said last time, all still true.

Chuck Eddy, Gavin Edwards, Jeff Pike, Steven Rubio, and Rob Sheffield always take time out from their own projects to support whatever I'm doing, something that especially mattered to me a couple of years ago.

Everyone at Huttonville P.S., as always (especially this year): Neil Ainger, Doug Chan, Susan Currie, Jeff Fraser, Anita Gormley, Amanda Hiscock, Andrew Hodgkinson, Theresa Iskra, Satpreet Jagpal, Krista Jarvie, Dianne Mann, Amy Morden, Jennifer Rollings, Sam & Andrea Sauro, Obe Vandertol, and Karen Watts.

I put out a book a couple of years ago that didn't sell much. The great thing about not selling books is that you can thank almost everyone individually who did buy a copy—J.K. Rowling can't do that. Adding to the names I've already listed: Evelyn Blackwell, Richard Cobeen, Jer Fairall, Lauren Huk, Paul Hum, Tasha Leona, Greg Morton, Erik Nelson, Vic Perry, Stefanie Poland, Gary Robertson, Tom Sawyer, Barb Wielocha, and Paul Woods. If I missed you, I'm sincerely sorry.

And for this, that, and the other, thanks to Jacqueline Baines, Vaughn Dragland, Pam & Dan Lavelle, Michaela Snow Parkinson, Geoff Savage, Gus Skarlatakis, Jack Thompson, Fred Ulrich, and Ava and Elliot Woods.

Phil and Scott would both like to thank Valerie Mais for her great work on the cover, and also Dave McMullen for comprising the entire readership of (and sometimes participating in) *Managing the Decay*, the website that started this whole project. One day, Dave, we promise that the lost podcast will be available as a virtual bootleg.

Scott Woods is a Business Analyst based in Toronto, the webmaster of GreilMarcus.net, and the producer of several non-award winning podcasts. He graciously accepts fan mail at scottmichaelwoods@gmail.com.

Phil Dellio retires in two years. He expects to be happy but lost.

Also by Phil & Scott:

I Wanna Be Sedated (Sound and Vision, 1993)
Quotable Pop (Sound and Vision, 2001)

Also by Phil:

Interrupting My Train of Thought (Createspace, 2014)

www.ingramcontent.com/pod-product-compliance
Lightning Source LLC
Chambersburg PA
CBHW070143290526
45789CB00002B/605